OhSewEasy®

life style

20 Projects to Make Your Home Your Own

Valori Wells & Carolyn Spencer

C&T PUBLISHING

Text and artwork copyright © 2008 by Valori Wells and Carolyn Spencer

Artwork copyright © 2008 by C&T Publishing, Inc.

Publisher: Amy Marson

Editorial Director: Gailen Runge

Acquisitions Editor: Jan Grigsby

Editor: Lynn Koolish

Technical Editors: Carol Zentgraf and Teresa Stroin

Copyeditor/Proofreader: Wordfirm Inc.

Cover/Book Designer: Kristen Yenche

Illustrator: Kirstie Pettersen

Production Coordinator: Zinnia Heinzmann

Photography by C&T Publishing, Inc., unless otherwise noted

Published by C&T Publishing, Inc., P.O. Box 1456, Lafayette, CA 94549

Wells, Valori.
  Oh sew easy. Life style : 20 projects to make your home your own / Valori Wells and Carolyn Spencer.
    p. cm.
  ISBN-13: 978-1-57120-444-8 (paper trade : alk. paper)
  ISBN-10: 1-57120-444-X (paper trade : alk. paper)
  1. Machine sewing. 2. Household linens. I. Spencer, Carolyn. II. Title.

TT713.W46 2008
646.2'044--dc22
                                        2007021724

Printed in China

10 9 8 7 6 5 4 3 2 1

Acknowledgments

First and foremost we would like to thank
Jean for her encouragement, knowledge, and
all the help as we learned to sew—we couldn't
have done this without you. A big thank-you to
Luke Mulks—you listened to our ideas, you saw
our vision and you made it happen. To our
husbands, thank you for your love and support
through all our ups and downs. To Olivia Rose,
for the little breaks that made us smile. We
would like to acknowledge all the C&T staff
for all of their hard work in making this book
so beautiful.

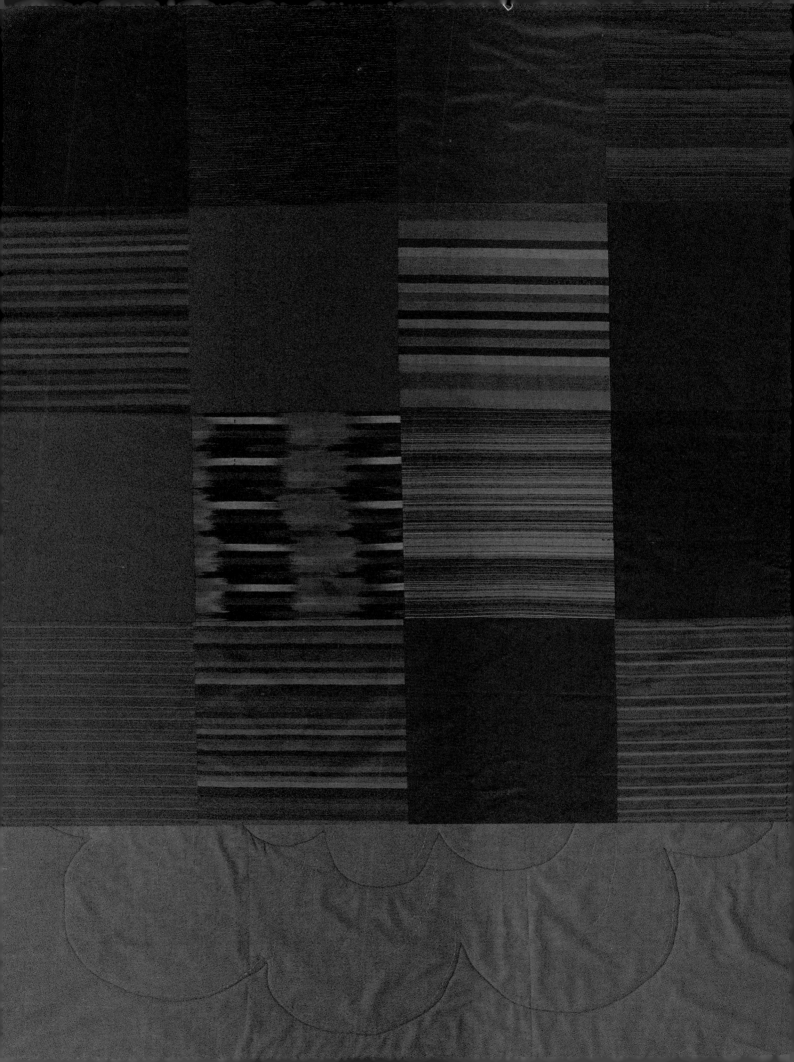

contents

introduction

Hello. We'd like to introduce ourselves. We are two young women who love to create accessories for everyday living. Val is an experienced quilter, and Carolyn is a beginner. Together, we've created stylish projects with color, function, and simplicity that you can make for your home or as gifts. Follow the projects as written, or use them as inspiration to make your own unique creations. All of the projects provide simple touches that will add a personalized look to any home or accessory.

Begin by reading the first chapter (Basic How-Tos) to get acquainted with the basic techniques used in the book. Then, look over the projects to select those that suit your lifestyle, or find a project that is the perfect gift. We've explored a variety of fabric styles and color palettes, so you're sure to find something that suits your style.

Most of all, we hope you enjoy creating projects that are uniquely *you* for your home and loved ones.

Valerie & Carolyn

basic how-tos

The following basic tools and techniques will help you create your projects in the best and simplest way possible. We've listed the tools we think you will need, but feel free to improvise and use what you have available. There is also a section with instructions for simple techniques that are used in a variety of the projects.

The Importance of Precision

It would be nice to think that every project you make will go according to plan, but let's face it—whether or not you are a beginner, things happen. However, two things will make your life a little less frustrating in the long run: accurate measuring and accurate cutting. Take the time to do these two things carefully, or your project will suffer and you will not be happy. In some cases, a glass of wine can also be very helpful, but too much can make matters worse!

To assist in your quest for accuracy, here are two techniques to help ensure that your projects will turn out straight, smooth, and accurate.

1. When you press fabric, be gentle. Steam and harsh movements can stretch and distort the fabric. In general, you want to press fabric with a vertical up-and-down motion, not by moving the iron across the fabric.

2. It is always good to pin projects to keep the edges aligned. Fabric can stretch and bunch if not pinned securely. You really can't use too many pins.

Sewing Must-Haves

■ **Scissors** Use a ruler and a chalk pencil to mark lines on the wrong side of the fabric; then use scissors to cut.

■ **Rotary Cutter** A rotary cutter has a very sharp, round blade mounted on a plastic handle, similar to a pizza cutter. It is available in several sizes. The medium-sized blade (45mm) is large enough for the projects in this book, while still being easy to handle. The rotary cutter is usually used with a rotary cutting ruler.

■ **Rotary Cutting Mat** This is a plastic, self-healing mat that protects the tabletop when you cut with a rotary cutter. It also helps keep the blade of your rotary cutter sharp. A 36″ × 24″ mat will be sufficient for the projects in this book.

■ **Rotary Cutting Ruler** These see-through acrylic rulers are marked in a grid pattern of 1″, ¾″, ½″, and ¼″. They are available in many different sizes. The sizes we used the most for the projects in this book were 6½″ × 24″ and 15″ × 15″. A 20½″ × 20½″ ruler is useful for the throws.

■ **Straight Pins** Fine, flat-head and glass-head pins are easier to see and use than are the long, thick-shank pins. Flat-head pins let you rest a rotary cutting ruler on top of pinned fabric. Glass-head pins won't melt under the heat of an iron.

■ **Seam Ripper** This can be your best friend and your worst enemy, but all in all, it is a must-have.

■ **Pencils** A fine mechanical pencil is helpful when marking light-colored fabric. A white chalk pencil is great for marking designs to embroider on the project top, because it will wash out, whereas a regular lead pencil will not.

■ **Flexible Tape Measure** This measuring tool is essential for accurate measuring when making piping and creating basket liners. (If you can't find one at your local quilt shop, check out an art supply store.)

■ **Stitching and Knitting Gauge** We use this handy little tool in many of our projects; it is not necessary but is very helpful. This is a 6″ metal ruler with a movable piece in the center, which allows you to set it at a specific measurement, such as ¼″ or ½″. This tool comes in handy when pressing down a seam allowance, as it allows you to keep the allowance measurement exact as you go.

■ **Embroidery Needles** A variety pack of different sizes is most useful; otherwise, get a small needle to whipstitch (see page 11) and a large-eyed needle for Big-Stitch Embroidery (see page 12) work.

■ **Sewing Machine** Make sure yours is in good working order. If your machine has a walking foot, it will come in very handy for putting together the throws. Follow the manufacturer's instructions for attaching the walking foot to the machine and for using it. Be sure to change the machine needle often, as it can get burrs and snag your fabric.

■ **Sewing Machine Needles** There are many different types of needles. We recommend sharps needles (sometimes called Microtex Sharps) in sizes 80/12 and 90/14. You can also use top-stitch needles in either size. When stitching heavier, decorator-weight fabrics, you will have better luck with a larger needle (90/14). It is very important to change your needle when you start a new project.

■ **Medium-Sized Safety Pins** These will come in handy when stitching the throws or the picnic cloths together; they will hold the layers together and keep the fabric from shifting.

■ **Thread** For basic stitching and piecing, we use 100% cotton thread in a neutral or matching color. For topstitching, we choose either a thread that matches the fabrics we are working with (which makes the topstitching disappear) or a contrasting thread (which creates a decorative line). Whichever you choose, it is very important that you use the same type of thread in the top of the machine as you do in the bobbin, so you will have the proper tension when you stitch. This will help you avoid lots of frustration and use of the seam ripper.

■ **Nonstick Appliqué Pressing Sheet** We use this sheet to protect our ironing board when fusing and when using fast2fuse Double-Sided Fusible Stiff Interfacing (see page 13).

■ **Finger Cots** These latex or rubber tubes slide over your fingers, allowing you to grip the needle better when doing Big-Stitch Embroidery or whipstitching.

Sewing Lingo

Selvage edges The edges of the fabric that run lengthwise and are tightly woven to prevent the edge from unraveling are called selvage edges. The name of the fabric manufacturer and colorful dots with numbers are often printed on the selvage edges.

Lengthwise grain The threads that run the length of the fabric parallel to the selvage edges are the lengthwise grain. There is very little stretch in this direction.

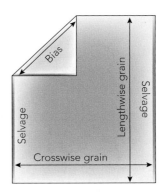

Grainlines and bias

Crosswise grain The threads that run across the width of the fabric from selvage edge to selvage edge are the crosswise grain. There is some stretch in this direction.

Lengthwise or crosswise grain is considered to be on-grain, or on the straight of grain.

Bias A 45° angle to the straight grain is called bias. Fabric cut on the bias is often used to make piping and bindings because the edges are stretchy and work well for curves and corners.

Seam allowance When stitching a seam, the seam allowance is the amount of fabric between the edge of the fabric and the stitching. Our standard seam allowance is ¼″, but a few projects use a ½″ seam allowance. Be sure to check the project instructions for the size of the seam allowance. Stitch seams with the fabric right sides together, unless otherwise indicated.

Back tack This stitch is used to reinforce the beginning and ending of a line of stitching. Put the machine into reverse, and stitch three or four stitches over the existing stitches. The project instructions will mention when it is really important to back tack.

Machine baste This stitch is used when making piping and when gathering fabric. Machine basting uses the longest stitch length on the machine.

Sewing Techniques
Stitching on Snaps

Be sure to use a double strand of thread; this will make stronger stitches that will last longer.

1. Thread a needle, double the strand, and knot the end.

2. Working from the back of the fabric, bring the needle up through one of the holes of the snap. Carry the thread over the metal edge, and stitch through the fabric to the back. Repeat 3 times, through the same hole.

3. Move to the next hole, and repeat Step 2 for the remaining holes.

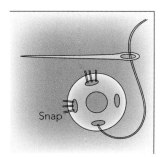

Stitch snaps through holes.

Whipstitch

Use a whipstitch to hand stitch openings closed.

1. Choose a high-quality thread in a color close to that of the fabrics you are using.

2. Use a single strand of thread, and make a knot at one end.

3. Stitch over the edges of the fabrics, securing them together.

4. When you reach the end of the opening that you are stitching closed, secure the thread by taking a few small stitches on top of each other. Trim off the excess thread.

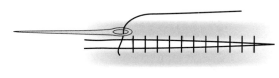

Whipstitch

Topstitch

When you stitch a seam, the stitching is hidden between the layers of fabric. Topstitching, however, is done on top of the fabric and is visible. It can be purely decorative, or it can help hold layers together. You can topstitch by hand or machine.

Satin Stitch

A satin stitch is made with wide zigzag stitches that are very close together. It is best to first test satin stitching on a piece of scrap fabric. Once you have it down, you can satin stitch your projects.

1. Refer to your sewing machine manual to find out what presser foot and what stitch length the manufacturer recommends for satin stitch; adjust your machine accordingly. You will need to adjust both the stitch length and the stitch width.

Tip

We set the stitch width at the widest setting that our machine allows and the stitch length to about 0.5 or 0.6. This creates more flexibility for the edges when making the organizers (pages 18–24). Test the stitch length and width to see what looks best for your project. When you test the stitch on a scrap of fabric, make sure that the stitching covers the edge of the fabric. If it doesn't, then you may need to make the stitches closer together (shorten the stitch length). The closer the stitches, the more the stitching will look like satin.

2. Set the needle to the far-right zigzag position, and align it with the edge of the piece you are stitching.

3. Begin stitching. Guide the fabric by looking in front of the presser foot.

Start with needle in far-right zigzag position.

4. To turn a corner, stitch right up to the end of the piece. Stop with the needle in the down position at the outside edge of the piece. Lift the presser foot, and pivot the fabric. Lower the foot, and resume stitching on the new edge.

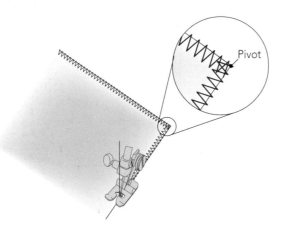

Stitch to corner, then pivot and continue stitching.

5. After you have satin stitched all the way around the piece, continue stitching over the starting point for ¼″ or back tack at both ends of the stitching to secure.

Big-Stitch Embroidery

For Big-Stitch Embroidery designs, you have unlimited options. Use a chalk pencil to create designs by tracing kitchen objects, drawing straight lines with a ruler, or printing lettering from the computer and tracing it onto fabric. Or, simply draw with the needle, and let the designs flow as you go. Either way, have fun, and remember that no matter how you design, each piece is a work of art that you created.

This stitch is simply a running stitch that uses all six strands of embroidery floss. Use a large-eye embroidery needle to stitch ⅛″-long running stitches spaced approximately ⅛″ apart. If you have a hard time gripping the needle, buy some finger cots (sold at your local fabric and/or quilting shop or at an office supply store).

That's it! This stitch is easy, decorative, and so fast.

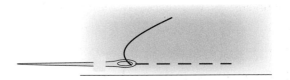

Big-Stitch Embroidery

Using Fusibles

We used several types of fusible products for the projects in this book. It is always a good idea to check the manufacturer's instructions for any specific requirements.

Lightweight Paper-Backed Fusible Web (Wonder-Under or Lite Steam-A-Seam)

We use fusible web to fuse layers of fabric together to make them stronger and more stable.

1. Draw the shape on the paper side (smooth side) of the fusible web, using a ruler to draw straight lines. Use paper scissors or a rotary cutter to cut out the shape slightly larger than drawn. As you cut, be sure to cut through both layers; do not separate the web from the paper.

2. Place the fabric right side down on the ironing board. Place the cut-out fusible web so that it is paper side up on the wrong side of the fabric—the rough, adhesive side of the web should be against the fabric.

3. Follow the manufacturer's instructions for iron temperature and steam or no steam. Place the iron on the paper backing and press. Don't slide the iron; simply press directly down and then lift up, holding down for about 5 seconds. Let the fabric cool.

4. Cut out the shape on the drawn line. Remove the paper backing. Place the adhesive side down on the other piece of fabric, and press with the iron to fuse in place.

fast2fuse Double-Sided Fusible Stiff Interfacing

For projects that need a little extra support, such as the organizers, we suggest fast2fuse Double-Sided Fusible Stiff Interfacing, as it is easy to use and provides just the right amount of stiffness.

1. Cut out the shapes as specified in the project instructions.

2. Place a nonstick appliqué pressing sheet on the ironing board, and then place the cut-out fast2fuse on top. Place the fabric right side up on top of the fast2fuse. Press with a hot, dry iron. For the larger pieces, start in the center of the piece, and press out to the edges until the entire surface of the fabric is adhered.

3. Turn the piece over, and place the second piece of fabric on the fast2fuse. Press with a hot, dry iron as in Step 2.

4. To permanently fuse the fabrics, press firmly with a hot iron and steam for 10 seconds on each side.

Tip

It's often easier to cut the fabric and fast2fuse a little larger than you need, and then trim to size after the fabric has been fused in place.

Fusible Interfacing

Fusible interfacing has the fusible glue on just one side. Follow the lightweight paper-backed fusible web instructions (previous page) to fuse fabric to the side of the interfacing that has the fusible glue.

Piping

Piping adds a finishing touch to pillows. Although you can buy premade piping, when you make your own you can select fabric that is the perfect accent for your pillow fabric. To make piping, you'll need cotton piping cording and fabric to make bias strips.

Making Piping

When purchasing cotton piping cording, buy enough to fit around the pillow perimeter plus 3″.

1. Use a flexible tape measure to measure around the cord. To determine the needed strip width, add ½″ to the measurement (enough for two ¼″ seam allowances).

2. For flexibility, cut fabric strips on the bias (see page 10). Place the ruler on a single layer of fabric at a 45° angle to the selvage, and cut several strips the required width.

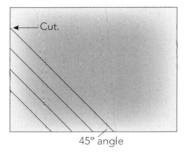

Cut fabric on bias.

3. Stitch the bias strips together end to end with diagonal seams. Press the seams open. Cut and add more strips until the length is the same as the length of the cord.

Join seams on diagonal.

4. Center the piping cord on the wrong side of the strip. Fold the strip over the cord, matching the raw edges. Use a zipper foot to machine baste close to the cord, starting and stopping 1½″ from each end.

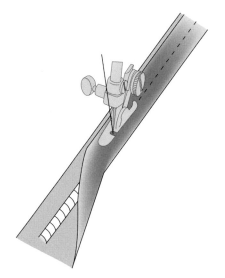

Stitch fabric around cord.

Pillows With Piping

1. Pin the piping to the right side of the pillow front, starting at the middle of one edge and matching the raw edges.

2. Clip into the piping seam allowance for a smooth turn at the corners. Start stitching 1½″ from one end of the cord. Stitch around the entire pillow, stopping 2½″ from the starting point.

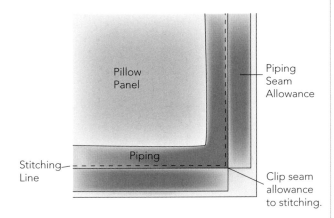

Clip piping.

3. Fold under the excess fabric strip, tucking it around the starting strip, and trim away the excess fabric. Cut the cording so the 2 ends butt together, and then stitch the final 4″.

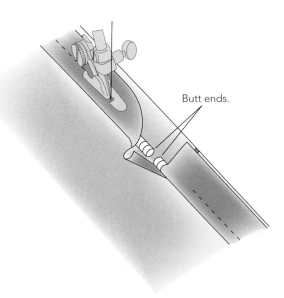

Join ends of piping.

4. Pin the pillow front to the back, right sides together. Use a zipper foot to stitch around the edges on the machine basting line. Leave one short edge open so you can insert the pillow form. Back tack at the starting and stopping points.

5. Trim the corners. Turn the cover right side out and press. Insert the pillow form, and whipstitch (page 11) the opening closed.

Envelope-Style Construction

Envelope-style construction is an easy way to finish edges for projects such as napkins, coasters, throws, and other items that are made from two or three layers of fabric.

1. Place the 2 or 3 pieces of fabric with right sides together. Pin the raw edges together.

2. Use a ¼″ seam allowance to stitch around the square, pivoting at the corners. To pivot, stop stitching ¼″ from the fabric edge with the needle in the down position. Lift the presser foot, and rotate the fabric a quarter turn. Lower the foot, and continue stitching the adjacent edge. Leave an opening in one edge (follow the specific project instructions to determine the size of the opening).

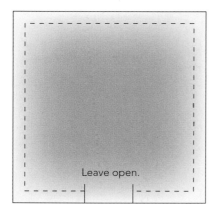

Leave open.

Envelope-Style Construction

Clean Finished-Edge Hem

Use a Clean Finished-Edge Hem when making aprons, totes, and more.

1. Unless a different hem width is specified, fold and press the edge ¼″ to the wrong side of the fabric.

2. Fold under ¼″ again and press. The raw edge will now be hidden.

3. Topstitch the center of the hem in place.

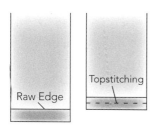

Raw Edge

Topstitching

Clean Finished-Edge Hem

Clean Edge Band

This technique is used for the apron waistbands and bag handles.

1. Fold the fabric strip in half lengthwise with the right side out. Press. This pressed line will be your guide.

Fold

Press fabric in half.

2. Open the fabric strip, and place it wrong side up. Using the pressed center line as a guide, fold each edge almost to the center. Press.

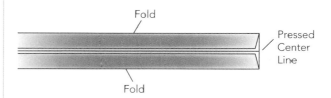

Fold

Pressed Center Line

Fold

Fold edges to center.

3. Fold the band in half again and press. All raw edges are now hidden.

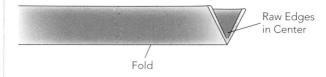

Raw Edges in Center

Fold

Finished Clean Edge Band

stylishly
organized

recipe or project organizer

Do you have stacks of recipes from friends and family or piles of cutouts from magazines? Here is a great way to organize them and keep them handy for quick reference. This organizer is perfect for those papers and projects that always seem to get lost. It is a great way to make a personalized gift. It's easy, fast, and oh so handy.

Materials

MATERIALS	YARDAGE	FOR
Cotton print	⅞ yard	Background and backing
Cotton solid	½ yard*	Pockets
Fusible web	½ yard	Pockets
fast2fuse	13″ × 42″	Background
Thread		Satin stitching
2 grommets		
Nonstick appliqué pressing sheet**		

If you are going to make each pocket a different color, you will need 2 rectangles 9″ × 6″ of each color for each pocket.

** Because the organizer is larger than a pressing sheet, either use multiple pressing sheets, or press one section at a time and then move the pressing sheet to the next section as you press.

Cutting

MATERIALS	CUTTING	FOR
Cotton print	2 @ 13″ × 42″	Background and backing
Cotton solid	8 @ 9″ × 6″*	Pockets
Fusible web	4 @ 9″ × 6″	Pockets
fast2fuse	1 @ 13″ × 42″	Background

If you are using different colors, cut 2 of each color for each pocket—front and back.

FINISHED SIZE: 13″ × 42″

Basic Sewing Techniques

- ■ Fusibles
- ■ Satin Stitch

Assembly

1. Fuse the background and backing fabrics to each side of the fast2fuse (page 13), right sides out and edges even.

2. To make each pocket, use fusible web (pages 12–13) to fuse 2 pocket fabric pieces together, right sides out and edges even. Make 4 pockets.

3. Satin stitch (pages 11–12) the top edge of each pocket.

4. Refer to the Pocket Layout (below), and use a ruler to place the pockets on the background, as shown. Pin the pockets in place.

5. Satin stitch the sides and bottom of each pocket to the background. Back tack at the starting and stopping point of each pocket.

6. Satin stitch around the edges of the background. Back tack at the starting and stopping point.

7. In each upper corner of the organizer, mark the grommet placement 1″ from the top edge and 1½″ from the side edge. Follow the manufacturer's instructions to attach the grommets at the marks.

Fill the organizer full of your favorite recipes, or collect all those papers for your ongoing projects.

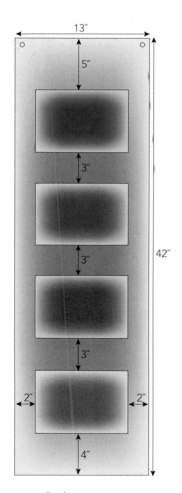

Pocket Layout

kid's day-of-the-week organizer

This colorful organizer is a fun way to teach kids the days of the week, while also giving them a place to put their favorite little toys. The organizer can also be made to hang vertically on the back of a door. Instead of days of the week, you can use colors, family names, animals, or shapes—there are so many possibilities. Have fun making one with a child, or make one to give as a gift.

Basic Sewing Techniques

- Fusibles
- Satin Stitch
- Big-Stitch Embroidery
- Topstitch

Materials

MATERIALS	YARDAGE	FOR
Cotton print	⅞ yard	Background, backing, and hanging loops
Cotton solid	⅜ yard*	Pockets
Fusible web	½ yard	Pockets
fast2fuse	10″ × 45″	Background
Thread		Satin stitching
Six-strand embroidery floss		Big-Stitch Embroidery
Embroidery needle		
Chalk pencil		
Nonstick appliqué pressing sheet**		

If you are going to make each pocket a different color, you will need 2 squares 5″x 5″ of each color for each pocket.

**Because the organizer is larger than the pressing sheet, either use multiple pressing sheets, or press one section at a time and then move the pressing sheet to the next section as you press.*

Cutting

MATERIALS	CUTTING	FOR
Cotton print	2 @ 10″ × 45″*	Background and backing
	5 @ 6″ × 6½″	Hanging loops
Cotton solid	14 @ 5″ × 5″	Pockets
Fusible web	7 @ 5″ × 5″	Pockets
fast2fuse	1 @ 10″ × 45″**	Background

Or cut as long of a piece as you can get after you cut off the selvage edges.

**Cut the same size as the background and backing.*

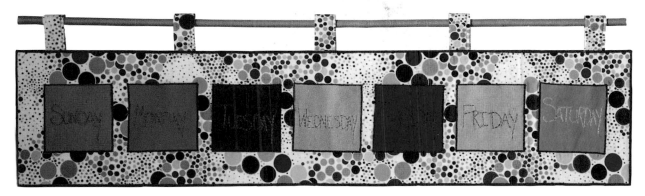

FINISHED SIZE: 45″ × 10″

Assembly

1. Use a chalk pencil to write the days of the week, or whatever words you choose, in the centers of 7 pocket squares. Use Big-Stitch Embroidery (page 12) to embroider the words.

2. Use fusible web (pages 12–13) to fuse each embroidered pocket square to a plain pocket square with right sides out and edges even. Make 7 pockets.

3. Satin stitch (pages 11–12) the top edge of each pocket.

4. To make each hanging loop, measure and press under ¼″ on the long edges of a 6″ × 6½″ rectangle. Fold and press the rectangle in half lengthwise, wrong sides together. Topstitch (page 11) the folded edges together ⅛″ from the edge.

5. Fold and press the loop in half crosswise with the short edges even. Baste the ends together ¼″ from the edge. Repeat Steps 4 and 5 to make 5 loops.

6. Fuse the background fabric with the pockets to the fast2fuse (page 13), right sides out and edges even.

7. Sandwich the hanging loops between the backing fabric and the fast2fuse as follows: Place the fast2fuse on an ironing board with the fabric side down. Place the backing fabric right side up on top of the fast2fuse with the edges even.

Slip the short ends of the hanging loops between the fast2fuse and the backing fabric. Make sure the loops are evenly spaced and all the same length. Fuse the fabric and the loops to the fast2fuse.

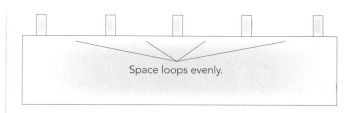

Space loops evenly.

Place loops between fabric and fast2fuse.

8. Refer to the Pocket Layout, and use a ruler to place the pockets on the background, as shown. Pin the pockets in place.

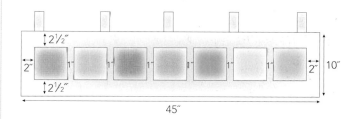

Pocket Layout

9. Satin stitch around the sides and bottom of each pocket. Back tack at the starting and stopping points of each pocket.

10. Satin stitch around the edges of the background. Stitch right over the loops to secure them. Stitch over the starting stitches to secure them.

Fill the pockets with your children's favorite toys, or their shoes and socks, and let them have fun learning the days of the week.

office organizer

FINISHED SIZE: 20″ × 28″

With today's busy, hectic schedules, we all need something to help us stay organized—something, anything, that can make our lives a little less frantic. This office organizer is designed to keep papers and files tidy and accessible, so you have one less pile to dig through. It also adds a stylish accent to your room.

Basic Sewing Techniques

- Fusibles
- Satin Stitch

Materials

MATERIALS	YARDAGE	FOR
Decorator print	1 yard	Background and backing
Decorator solid	½ yard	Pockets
Fusible web	½ yard	Pockets
fast2fuse	20″ × 28″	Background
Thread		Satin stitching
3 grommets		
Nonstick appliqué pressing sheet*		

Because the organizer is larger than the pressing sheet, either use multiple pressing sheets, or press one section at a time and then move the pressing sheet to the next section as you press.

Cutting

MATERIALS	CUTTING	FOR
Decorator print	2 @ 20″ × 28″	Background and backing
Decorator solid	4 @ 15″ × 7½″	Pocket fronts
	4 from template pattern A*	Pocket sides
Fusible web	2 @ 15″ × 7½″	Pockets
fast2fuse	20″ × 28″	Background

Template pattern A is on page 24.

Assembly

1. To make each pocket, use fusible web (pages 12–13) to fuse 2 pocket front pieces together with right sides out and edges even. Make 2 pocket fronts.

2. Satin stitch (pages 11–12) the side pieces to the short edges of each pocket front, with the side pieces right side up. Satin stitch the top edges of the pocket sides and fronts.

Satin stitch pocket side to pocket front.

3. Press each side piece in half lengthwise, right sides together.

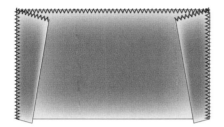

Press side pieces in half.

4. Refer to the Pocket Layout, and use a ruler to place the pockets on the background, as shown. Pin the pockets in place.

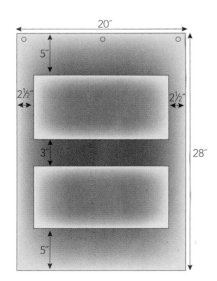

Pocket Layout

5. Start with a back tack, and satin stitch the back folded edges of the pocket sides to the background fabric (right sides up), holding the front edges of the sides out of the way as you stitch. Make sure that when the pocket is folded, the satin-stitched front edges align with the satin-stitched back edges.

6. Satin stitch the bottom edge of each pocket to the background. Back tack at the starting and stopping point of each pocket.

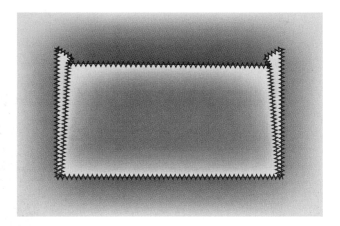

Satin stitch sides first, then bottom.

7. Fuse the background (with the pockets) and backing fabrics to the fast2fuse (page 13).

8. Satin stitch around the entire background. Back tack at the starting and stopping points.

9. Mark the grommet placement 1″ from the top and 1½″ from the sides. Add a third grommet in the center. Follow the manufacturer's instructions to attach the grommets at the marks.

Hang your organizer, and feel in control.

Pocket Sides Template
Pattern A

catch-all basket liners

Baskets provide an easy way to add a cozy touch to your home. They're attractive and useful. But sometimes a plain basket just doesn't do the job. If you're a knitter, you don't want your yarn to get caught on the reeds. If you're using your basket to store shoes, you need something to catch the dirt and keep it from getting on the floor. When you use a basket for laundry, you don't want your clothes getting snagged. Our solution: easy basket liners! We'll show you how to make liners for any shape or size basket.

FINISHED SIZE: Custom fit

Basic Sewing Techniques

- Satin Stitch

- Topstitch

Materials

Fabric requirements will depend on the size of basket (see next page).

Ribbon the length of the perimeter of the top rim of the basket plus 18˝

Flexible tape measure

Pencil

Paper

Stitching and knitting gauge

Fabric Requirements
Rectangular or Square Basket Liner

MEASURE (refer to illustrations below)	EXAMPLE
1. Use a flexible tape measure to measure 2 adjacent sides of the basket at the basket's largest point, usually the top rim.	38″
2. Add ½″ to this measurement to determine the cut length of the side pieces.	38½″
3. Measure the height of the basket.	14″
4. Add 5″ to the height to determine the cut height of the side pieces.	19″
5. Measure 2 adjacent sides of the bottom of the basket.	21″ × 17″
6. Add ½″ to each side to determine the cut size for the bottom piece.	21½″ × 17½″
7. Create the Cutting Layout.	
DETERMINE YARDAGE (refer to Cutting Layout below)	
1. Measure the width of the fabric.	40″
2. Start with the cut length of the 2 side pieces.*	38½″
3. Add the length of the bottom piece.	+ 17½″ = 56″
4. Divide by 36″ (the number of inches in a yard).	= 1.56 yards
5. Round up to the next quarter yard.	1.75 (1¾) yards

If both side pieces will not fit in the width of the fabric, add 2 times the cut width of the side pieces, for example 38½″ × 2.

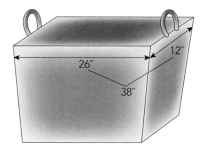

Measure 2 adjacent sides of basket at widest point.

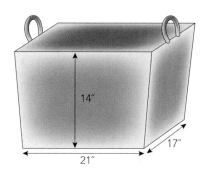

Measure height of basket.

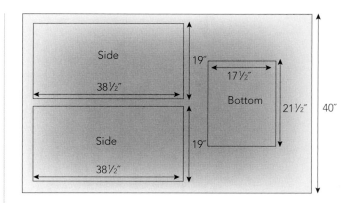

Create Cutting Layout to determine yardage.

Oh Sew Easy Life Style

Round Basket Liner

MEASURE (refer to illustrations below)	EXAMPLE
1. Use a flexible tape measure to measure the perimeter of the basket at its largest point, usually the top rim.	55″
2. Divide by 2, and then add ½″ to determine the cut length of the side pieces.	27½″ + ½″ = 28″
3. Measure the height of the basket.	11″
4. Add 4″ to the height to determine the cut height of the side pieces.	15″
5. Measure the diameter of the widest part (either the top or bottom edge) of the basket. Add ½″ to determine the cut diameter of the bottom piece.	17¼″ + ½″ = 17¾″
6. Create the Cutting Layout.	
DETERMINE YARDAGE (refer to Cutting Layout below)	
1. Measure the width of the fabric.	40″
2. Start with the cut length of the 2 side pieces.*	28″
3. Add the diameter of the bottom piece.	+ 17¾″
4. Divide by 36″ (the number of inches in a yard).	= 1.27 yards
5. Round up to the next third of a yard.	1.33 (1⅓) yards

If both side pieces will not fit in the width of the fabric, add 2 times the cut length of the side pieces, for example, 28″ x 2.

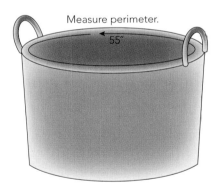

Measure perimeter of basket at widest point.

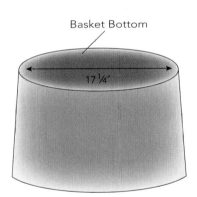

Measure diameter of bottom.

Measure height of basket.

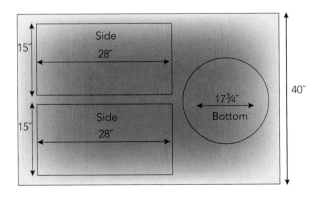

Create Cutting Layout to determine yardage.

Assembly

Seam allowances are ¼".

Rectangular or Square Basket

1. Refer to the chart on page 26 to measure the basket, determine yardage, and make a Cutting Layout for a rectangular or square basket.

2. Cut 2 rectangles for the liner sides and 1 rectangle for the liner bottom.

3. Place the 2 side pieces right sides together, and stitch together the side pieces along one short edge. To mark the drawstring opening on the unsewn short edge, measure down 1½" from the top edge, and mark with a pencil. Then, measure down 2½" from the top edge, and make another pencil mark.

4. To stitch the seam, begin at the top edge, and stitch to the first mark. Stop, back tack, lift the presser foot, and start stitching again at the second mark. Back tack, and then stitch the rest of the seam. Press the side seams open.

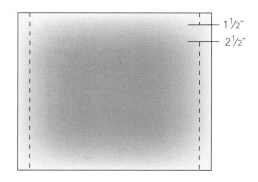

Mark drawstring opening, and stitch.

5. To make the drawstring casing, press under ½" on the top edge. Then press under another 1" on the top edge. Topstitch (page 11) along the bottom fold of the casing.

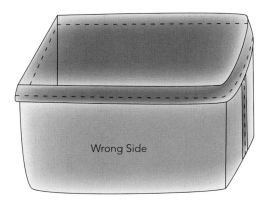

Topstitch along bottom of casing.

6. Fold the bottom piece in half lengthwise. Mark each end of the fold with a pin.

Fold bottom piece and mark center with pins.

7. Pin the short sides to the bottom piece, with right sides together and matching the side seams and the pin marks. Pin ¼" from each end.

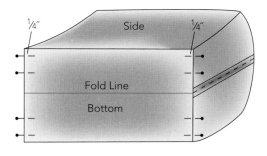

Match fold line on bottom to short side seams and pin.

8. Stitch the short edges of the bottom to the sides. Start and stop stitching ¼" from the corners.

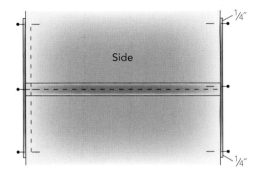

Start and stop stitching ¼" from corners of bottom piece.

9. Pin the remaining edges of the bottom piece to the edges of the sides, right sides together. Stitch together, starting and ending ¼" from the corners.

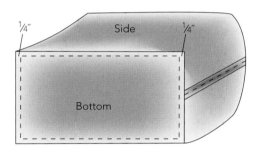

Stitch remaining sides.

10. If the basket has handles like ours, measure the outside width of the handle. Our handle measured 6½".

Measure width of handle.

11. On the seamed sides of the liner, measure and mark the height of the basket across the seamline. Mark the handle width centered across the seam.

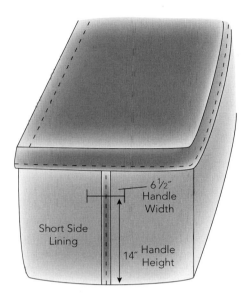

Measure and mark basket height and handle width on lining.

12. Use a pair of sharp fabric scissors to cut on the marked Handle Width line.

13. Satin stitch (pages 11–12) around the cut edges.

14. Fasten a safety pin to one end of the ribbon. Push the closed safety pin through the opening of the drawstring casing. Continue pushing the safety pin through the casing until the end of the ribbon comes out where you started.

15. Put the liner over the basket handles, and fit the lining into the basket. Pull the ribbon ends tightly and tie.

Round Basket

1. Refer to the chart on page 27 to measure the basket, determine yardage, and make a Cutting Layout for a round basket.

2. Cut the 2 rectangles for the sides and the circle for the bottom.

3. Stitch together the short edges of the side pieces to form a tube.

4. On the wrong side of the fabric, measure down ½″ from the top edge. Fold and press. Then measure from the top edge to fold down another 1″. Press.

Make first fold at ½″.

5. Topstitch (page 11) along the bottom fold of the casing.

Topstitch along bottom of casing.

6. Fold the bottom piece in half, right sides together, and mark both ends of the fold with a pin. Open the fabric, and fold in half again, matching the pins. Mark each end of the fold with a pin.

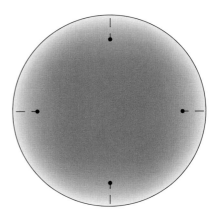

Mark quarter points with pins.

7. Fold the tube in half, matching seamlines, and mark each side of the fold on the bottom edge with pins. Pin the bottom piece to the tube, with right sides together and matching the pins on the bottom piece to the seamlines and to the pins on the tube.

8. Start stitching just past one of the seamlines of the tube. Stitch slowly, lining up the edges as you go. The fabric will ease better if you don't pin all the way around the bottom.

Tip

If your basket is small, you may want to make ⅛″-deep clips along the edge of the bottom circle to ease the seam. Make the clips about ¼″ apart, and be sure you don't clip into the seamline.

9. If your basket doesn't have handles, place the liner in the basket, and fold the edge over the top.

10. If your basket has handles, measure the outside width of the handle. (Our basket handle measures 7″.)

Measure width of basket handle.

11. At each side seam, measure and mark the height and width of the handle across the seamline.

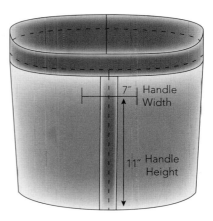

Measure and mark handle height and width on liner.

12. Use a pair of sharp fabric scissors to cut on the marked Handle Width line.

13. Satin stitch (pages 11–12) around the cut edges.

14. Put the liner over the handles of the basket, and push it into the basket.

stylishly
functional

sassy aprons

Aprons were created for a purpose—to keep your clothes clean while cooking. Well, that was then, and this is now. We've seen how aprons have become more of an accessory. Stores have them in a variety of colors and styles, with some beaded and others more practical—and we want them all.

So here's the perfect balance. These sassy aprons can be made as gifts or for yourself. They can be perfectly practical in every way or as sassy as sassy gets. Plan a cocktail party, put on your favorite little black dress, and complete your outfit with a cocktail apron. You'll be the hit of the night!

Basic Sewing Techniques

- Clean Edge Band
- Whipstitch
- Topstitch
- Clean Finished-Edge Hem

FINISHED SIZES:

KITCHEN APRON: 28″ long

COCKTAIL APRON: 23″ long

Materials

MATERIALS	YARDAGE	FOR
Cotton print 1	¾ yard	Main body
Cotton print 2	¼ yard	Top band and pockets
Cotton print 3	½ yard	Waistband
Thread		Topstitching
Buttons, rickrack, ribbon, or beads		Accents
Stitching and knitting gauge (optional)		

Cutting

MATERIALS	CUTTING	FOR
Cotton print 1	1 @ 30½″ × 20½″	Main body (kitchen apron)
	1 @ 30½″ × 15½″	Main body (cocktail apron)
Cotton print 2	1 @ 5½″ × 18½″	Top band
	4 @ 5½″ × 5½″	Pockets
Cotton print 3	2 @ 6″ × width of fabric	Waistband

Assembly

Waist Band

1. Cut off the selvage edges from the 2 strips of waistband fabric. Use a ½″ seam allowance to stitch together the short ends of the waistband strips to make one long strip. Press the seam open.

2. Measure and press under ¼″ on the short edges of the waistband strip. Make the waistband as a Clean Edge Band (page 15).

Pockets

1. To round the bottom corners of each pocket, place 2 pocket squares right sides together, and fold in half. Use a chalk pencil to draw a quarter circle in the corner of the raw edges. Cut on the chalk line through all layers.

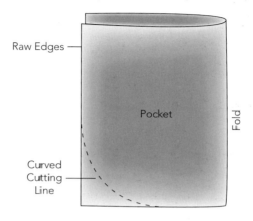

Round the pocket corners.

2. For each pocket, open the fold, and stitch the pieces together, using a ¼˝ seam allowance. Leave a 3˝ opening in the center of the top edge.

3. Trim the points from each corner. Be sure not to cut so close that you cut the stitching. Make ⅛˝-deep clips along the curved edge so the seam will be smooth when the pocket is turned right side out.

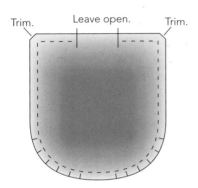

Trim corners and clip curve.

4. Turn each pocket right side out and press, pressing under the seam allowance of the opening. Whipstitch (page 11) the opening closed.

Top Band

Make a Clean Finished-Edge Hem (page 15) on the short edges of the rectangle.

Main Body

1. Make a Clean Finished-Edge Hem around the entire main body of the apron.

2. Pin the pockets to the main body 2½˝ from the sides and 2½˝ from the top edge.

3. Topstitch each pocket to the main body, stitching ⅛˝ from the edges of the pocket. Leave the top edge open.

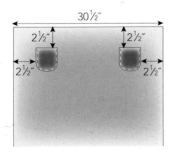

Place and topstitch pockets.

Tip

When choosing a thread for the topstitching, you can choose a color that blends perfectly with the fabric or a contrasting color so that the topstitching becomes a decorative touch.

4. To make a gathering stitch, set the machine stitch length to the longest stitch (usually 5). Stitch across the top edge of the main body piece, ¾˝ from the edge.

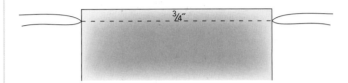

Gathering stitch

5. Remove the fabric from the machine, and cut the threads, leaving long tails. Knot the thread tails together at one end of the stitching. At the opposite end, gently pull the bobbin thread (the bottom thread) to gather the main body until it is the same length as the top band (18½˝). Even out the gathers. Knot the thread tails together to secure.

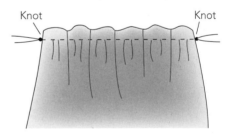

Pull threads to gather edge.

6. Set the sewing machine back to a normal stitch length.

Put the Apron Together

1. Fold the top band in half crosswise, and mark the bottom edge of the fold with a pin. Fold the top edge of the gathered main body in half, and mark the fold with a pin.

2. Place the top edge of the main body on the bottom edge of the top band, with right sides up. Overlap the edges 1″, and match the center pins. Pin the overlapped edges together.

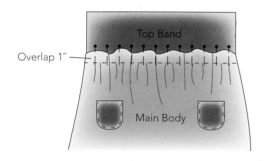

Place main body over bottom edge of top band.

3. Topstitch the main body to the top band along the gathering stitch line.

4. Press under ½″ on the top edge of the top band, and then open the fold. The pressed line will be your guide as you insert the edge into the waistband.

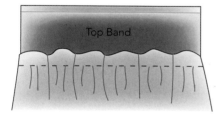

Fold and mark.

5. Fold the top band and the main body in half crosswise and mark the center of the top edge with a pin. Fold the waistband in half crosswise and mark the center of the bottom (open) edge with a pin.

6. Place the top edge of the top band in the open edges of the waistband. Match the center pins, and align the pressed line on the top band with the bottom edges of the waistband. Pin the layers together. Topstitch along the bottom edge of the waistband.

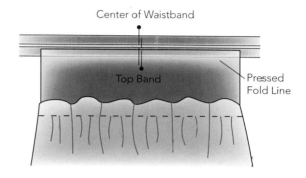

Align centers.

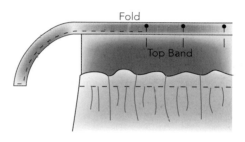

Topstitch around waistband.

7. Add trims and embellishments as desired to match your fabrics.

anywhere you go apron

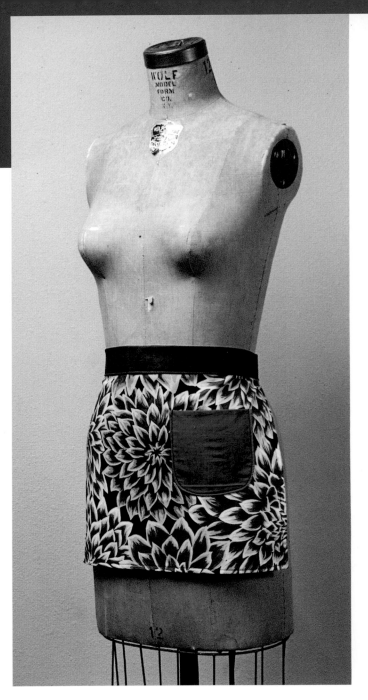

Sister to the Sassy Apron, the Anywhere You Go Apron is designed to be worn as a fashion accessory. It's modern, it's hip, and it's ready to go where you go. Step it up as you step out!

Basic Sewing Techniques

- Clean Edge Band
- Whipstitch
- Topstitch
- Clean Finished-Edge Hem

Materials

MATERIALS	YARDAGE	FOR
Cotton print 1	½ yard	Main body
Cotton print 2	¼ yard	Pocket
Cotton solid	½ yard	Waistband
Thread		Topstitching
Buttons, rickrack, ribbon, or beads		Accents
Stitching and knitting gauge (optional)		

Cutting

MATERIALS	CUTTING	FOR
Cotton print 1	1 @ 19½″ × 13½″	Main body
Cotton print 2	2 @ 5½″ × 5½″	Pocket
Cotton solid	2 @ 6″ × width of fabric	Waistband

Assembly

Waistband

1. Cut off the selvage edges from the 2 strips of waistband fabric. Use a ½" seam allowance to stitch together the short ends of the waistband strips to make one long strip. Press the seam open.

2. Measure and press under ¼" on the short edges of the waistband strip. Make the waistband as a Clean Edge Band (page 15).

Pocket

1. To round the bottom corners of the pocket, place the 2 pocket squares right sides together, and fold in half. Use a chalk pencil to draw a quarter circle in the corner of the raw edges. Cut on the chalk line through all the layers.

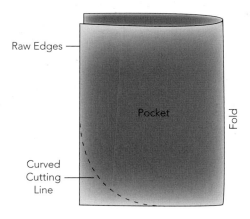

Round the pocket corners.

2. Open the fold, and stitch the pieces together, using a ¼" seam allowance. Leave a 3" opening in the center of the top edge.

3. Trim the points from each corner. Be sure not to cut so close that you cut the stitching. Make ⅛"-deep clips around the curved edge so the seam will be smooth when the pocket is turned right side out.

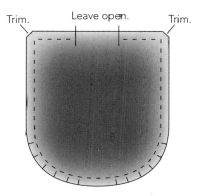

Trim corners and clip curve.

4. Turn the pocket right side out and press, pressing under the seam allowance of the opening. Whipstitch (page 11) the opening closed.

Main Body

Make a Clean Finished-Edge Hem (page 15) on both short edges and one long edge of the main body of the apron.

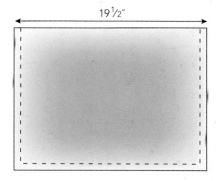

Clean finish and topstitch.

Put the Apron Together

1. Press under ½″ on the top edge of the main body, and then open the fold. The pressed line will be your guide as you insert the edge in the waistband. Fold the body in half crosswise, and mark the center fold with a pin.

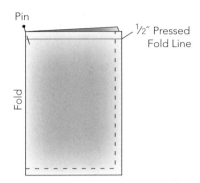

Fold and mark.

2. Fold the waistband in half crosswise and mark the center of the bottom (open) edge with a pin.

3. Place the top edge of the main body in the open edges of the waistband. Match the center pins, and align the pressed line on the top of the main body with the bottom edges of the waistband. Pin the layers together.

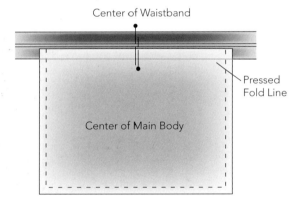

Align centers.

4. Topstitch around the entire waistband.

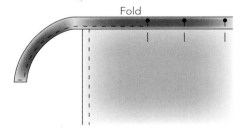

Topstitch around waistband.

5. Pin the pocket to the apron 2″ from either side edge and 4½″ from the top edge.

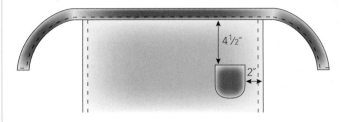

Pocket Placement

6. Topstitch the pocket to the apron, stitching ⅛″ from the edges of the pocket. Leave the top edge open.

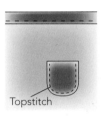

Topstitch pocket.

Slap on a pair of jeans and your new apron, and go out on the town!

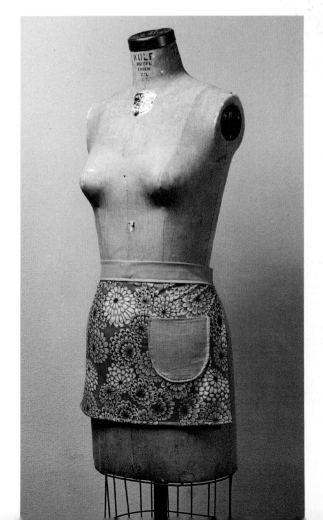

picnic cloth

Don't you just love picnics in the park or out in the country? Who needs a picnic table when you have your own picnic cloth? Keep it folded in the back of your car, ready for an impromptu lunch. It's simple, it's stylish, it's practical—what more could you ask for?

Basic Sewing Techniques

- Big-Stitch Embroidery
- Whipstitch
- Envelope-Style Construction

Photo by Valori Wells

FINISHED SIZE: $72\frac{1}{2}'' \times 72\frac{1}{2}''$

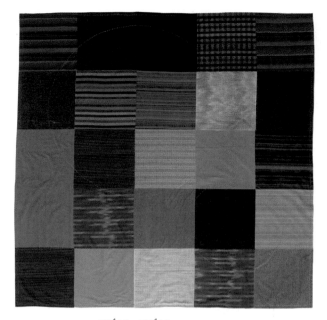
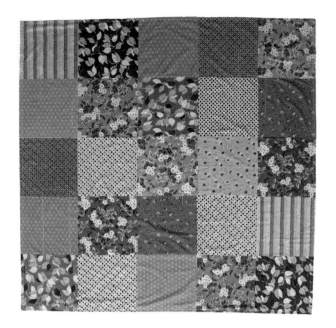

FINISHED SIZE: $72\frac{1}{2}" \times 72\frac{1}{2}"$

Materials

MATERIALS	YARDAGE	FOR
13 different cotton prints	½ yard each	Top
Cotton fabric 1	3½ yards	Backing sides
Cotton fabric 2	1 yard	Backing center
Six-strand embroidery floss		
Embroidery needle		
Finger cots for embroidery (optional)		
15" × 15" square ruler (optional)		

Cutting

MATERIALS	CUTTING	FOR
13 different cotton prints	2 @ 15" × 15" from each (you will have 1 left over)	Top
Cotton fabric 1	4 @ 29¼" × width of fabric	Backing sides
Cotton fabric 2	2 @ 15½" × width of fabric	Backing center

Assembly

Seam allowances are ¼".

1. For this project, use a design wall or the floor. Refer to the Front Layout to arrange the 15" squares into 5 rows of 5 squares each. Move the squares around until you like the arrangement. You will have 1 square left over.

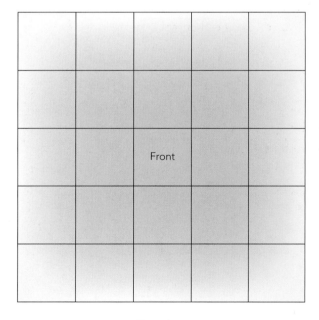

Front Layout

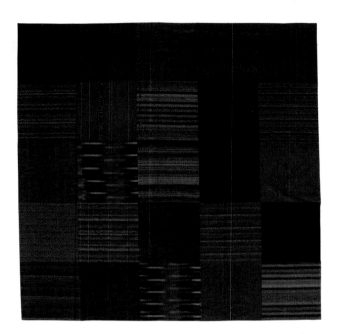

2. Stitch together the squares in each row.

3. Press the seam allowances for each row in alternate directions so the seams nest when you stitch the rows together.

4. Pin the first row to the second. Nest the seams of opposite blocks, pinning at the seams. Stitch row 1 to row 2.

5. Repeat Step 4 to pin and stitch row 2 to row 3, row 3 to row 4, and then row 5 to row 4. You now have a complete top.

6. Press the top, and set it aside.

7. Cut off the selvage edges from the backing pieces. Stitch together the short edges of 2 backing side pieces. Repeat for the 2 remaining backing side pieces and the 2 backing center pieces. Press the seams in alternating directions.

8. Refer to the Backing Layout, and stitch the panels together, matching the center seams.

Backing Side	Backing Center	Backing Side

Backing Layout

9. Press the backing, and then place it on the floor right side up. Center the pieced top right side down on the backing, and trim the backing edges even with the edges of the top.

Note: If the top is wider than the backing, don't panic! Piece the extra fabric that was trimmed from the backing ends, as needed, to make a strip long enough to go down the side. Stitch the added strip to the backing, and then press.

10. Place the backing and the pieced top right sides together. If you added an extra strip to make the backing larger, trim it even with the edge of the pieced top. Pin the pieced top to the backing around the edges and in the center.

11. Use Envelope-Style Construction (pages 14–15) to stitch together the top and the backing. Leave a 15″ opening.

12. Trim the points from each corner. Be sure not to cut so close that you cut the stitching.

13. Turn the picnic cloth right side out. Slide your fingers in the opening to push the seams to the edges. Press. Work your way around the picnic cloth until all the edges are pressed. Press under the seam allowances of the opening.

14. Use large safety pins to pin the layers together. Pin every other square to keep the top secured to the backing as you embroider.

15. Use Big-Stitch Embroidery (page 12) to stitch the layers together. Choose an embroidery floss color that complements the picnic cloth—you can match the floss to the pieced top, or you can use a contrasting color to make the stitches stand out. If you want to hide the knots, the 15″ opening will stay open until the end, so you can start each new line of stitching from between the layers.

Begin by starting at the opening and stitching around the picnic cloth, ½″ from the edge, knotting off and starting new pieces of embroidery floss as needed. If you like, you can add decorative stitching to help hold the layers together. Finish by completing the edge stitching at the 15″ opening.

16. Whipstitch (page 11) the opening closed.

The picnic cloth is ready for use. Choose your favorite spot, pack a lunch, and enjoy!

picnic silverware pocket

Complete the picnic set with this handy holder for your picnic silverware. Make one just for picnics, make several to store your special-occasion silverware, or complete the perfect wedding or anniversary gift with this unique personalized accessory.

Basic Sewing Techniques

- Stitching on Snaps
- Topstitch
- Whipstitch

Materials

MATERIALS	YARDAGE	FOR
Cotton fabric 1	½ yard	Inside
Cotton fabric 2	½ yard	Outside
Rickrack	½ yard	Embellishment
Ribbon	1 yard	Tie
1 Snap		
1 Button		
Chalk pencil		

FINISHED SIZE: 12½″ × 19½″ (open) with six 2″ × 4″ pockets

Cutting

MATERIALS	CUTTING	FOR
Cotton fabric 1	13″ × 20″	Inside
	13″ × 9″	Pocket
Cotton fabric 2	13″ × 20″	Outside

Assembly

Seam allowances are ¼".

1. Press the 13" × 9" pocket piece in half lengthwise, wrong sides together.

2. Measure and pin the rickrack across the folded pocket, 1" from the folded edge. Topstitch (page 11) in place.

3. Pin the pocket to the inside piece, with right sides up, aligning the raw edges of the pocket with the bottom and side edges of the inside piece. Topstitch the pocket in place about ¼" from the raw edges, leaving the top edge open. Back tack at the starting and stopping points.

4. To create the pocket divisions, measure 2½" from each side edge, and use a chalk marker to draw a line. Draw 3 more lines, spaced 2" apart, between the outer lines. Topstitch along each line. Back tack at the top and bottom of the pockets.

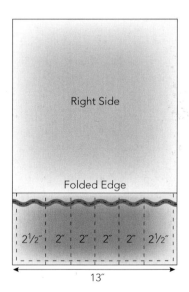

Right Side

Folded Edge

| 2½" | 2" | 2" | 2" | 2" | 2½" |

13"

Pocket Placement

5. Stitch the snap base (page 11) to the right side of the outside piece 1½" up from the center of the bottom edge.

6. Fold the ribbon in half. Measure 5" from the bottom of the inside piece, and pin the fold of the ribbon to the left edge.

7. Place the outside and inside piece right sides together with the ribbon sandwiched between the fabric layers. Be sure the end of the outside piece with the

snap is aligned with the pocket end of the inside piece. Stitch the 2 pieces together, leaving a 2" opening on one side. Turn the silverware holder right side out. Press, pressing under the seam allowances of the opening. Slide your fingers in the opening, and push the seams to the edges.

8. Whipstitch (page 11) the opening closed.

9. Use contrasting thread (or a matching color if you don't want your stitching to show) to topstitch around the holder ¼" from the edges.

10. Stitch the top part of the snap to the inside of the silverware holder 1" from the center of the top edge.

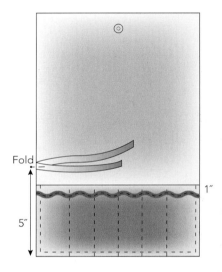

Fold

1"

5"

Ribbon and Snap Placement

11. Stitch the button to the outside of the silverware holder so it covers the snap stitches.

Fill the holder with your picnic silverware, fold it over, snap it shut, and enjoy your picnic.

napkins and coasters

Napkins and coasters are so easy to make. Why not make a bunch so you can match your favorite table-cloth, have a set to go with your picnic cloth, and keep some cocktail coasters just for fun.

The Picnic Napkin is a standard-size dinner napkin, which makes it very versatile. The cocktail napkin is perfect for any party. It's just the right size to catch those drink dribbles. The coasters will keep the drips off your furniture.

Cocktail Coasters

FINISHED SIZES:

COCKTAIL COASTERS: 4″ × 4″

COCKTAIL NAPKINS: 8″ × 8″

PICNIC NAPKINS: 16″ × 16″

Cocktail Napkins

Picnic Napkins

Basic Sewing Techniques

- Envelope-Style Construction
- Whipstitch
- Big-Stitch Embroidery (optional)
- Topstitch

Materials

Picnic Napkins

MATERIALS	YARDAGE	FOR
Cotton print	2 yards	4 picnic napkins
OR		
2 cotton prints	1 yard each	4 reversible picnic napkins
Thread		Topstitching

Cocktail Napkins

MATERIALS	YARDAGE	FOR
Cotton print	⅝ yard	4 cocktail napkins
OR		
2 cotton prints	⅓ yard each	4 reversible cocktail napkins
Thread		Topstitching

Cocktail Coasters

MATERIALS	YARDAGE	FOR
Cotton solid	⅜ yard*	9 cocktail coasters
	OR	
	¼ yard each	9 reversible cocktail coasters
Six-strand embroidery floss		
Embroidery needle		
Finger cots (optional)		
Chalk pencil (optional)		
Decorative accents, such as rickrack or beads (optional)		

If you prefer, choose several colors to mix and match the fronts and backs and adjust your yardage accordingly.

Cutting

Picnic Napkins

MATERIALS	CUTTING	FOR
Cotton print	8 @ 16½" × 16½"	Picnic napkins

Cocktail Coasters

MATERIALS	CUTTING	FOR
Cotton solid	18 @ 4½" × 4½"	Cocktail coasters

Cocktail Napkins

MATERIALS	CUTTING	FOR
Cotton print	8 @ 8½" × 8½"	Cocktail napkins

Assembly

Seam allowances are ¼".

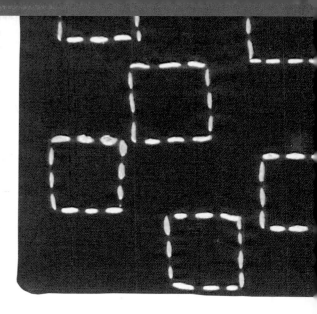

The Picnic and Cocktail Napkins are stitched together as described below. For the Cocktail Coasters, we used Big-Stitch Embroidery before stitching the pieces together to create the imperfect stitched squares. We chose this design to match the martini glasses we planned to use for our party. You can do the same or change the design to complement your own style. If you choose to do Big-Stitch Embroidery, be sure that you embroider all the tops of the coasters before stitching them to the backs so the knots will be hidden.

1. If desired, add Big-Stitch Embroidery (page 12) to one or both fabric squares for each coaster.

2. For each napkin or coaster, pin 2 squares (a top and a bottom) with right sides together. Use Envelope-Style Construction (pages 14–15) to stitch them together. Leave a 2" opening.

3. Trim the points from each corner. Be sure not to cut so close that you cut the stitching. Turn right side out.

4. Slide your fingers into the opening, and push the seams to the edges. Press, pressing under the seam allowances of the opening.

5. Whipstitch (page 11) the opening closed.

6. Set the machine stitch length to the longest stitch (usually 5). Topstitch ½" from the edge around the entire napkin or coaster.

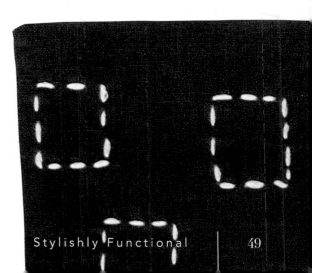

travel or diaper tote

These totes are great for travel or for carrying the baby's essentials when you are out and about. The smaller-size tote also makes a great purse for a woman who likes to have everything with her. It's ideal for knitting projects, a sketchbook and pencils, or whatever you carry with you. These totes are made using a heavier-weight fabric so that they are durable as well as stylish.

Basic Sewing Techniques

- Fusibles

- Clean Edge Band

- Clean Finished-Edge Hem

- Topstitch

Materials

We used a heavier-weight decorator fabric for the outside of the bag and a lighter-weight fabric for the lining. You can choose to make the whole bag out of a lighter-weight cotton, if you like. Decorator fabric can range from 42″ wide to 54″ wide; we based our yardage on fabric that is 42″ wide.

FINISHED SIZES:

DIAPER TOTE: $12\frac{1}{2}″ \times 8\frac{1}{2}″ \times 4″$

TRAVEL TOTE: $18″ \times 12″ \times 4″$

Diaper Tote

MATERIALS	YARDAGE	FOR
Decorator fabric	1 yard	Outside of tote
Lining fabric	⅔ yard	Lining
Fusible interfacing– 22″ wide	⅞ yard	
12″ zipper		
Thread to match outside fabric		

Travel Tote

MATERIALS	YARDAGE	FOR
Decorator fabric	1⅝ yards	Outside of tote
Lining fabric	1 yard	Lining
Fusible interfacing–22″ wide	1⅜ yards	
18″ zipper		
Thread to match outside fabric		
Chalk pencil		

Cutting
Diaper Tote

MATERIALS	CUTTING	FOR
Decorator fabric	2 @ 5″ × 13½″	Bottom and top
	2 @ 5″ × 9½″	Sides
	2 @ 9½″ × 13½″	Front and back
	2 @ 6″ × 25″	Handles
	2 @ 5″ × 7½″	Side pockets
	1 @ 7½″ × 13½″	Back pocket
Lining fabric	1 @ 5″ × 13½″	Bottom
	2 @ 5″ × 9½″	Sides
	2 @ 9½″ × 13½″	Front and back
	2 @ 5″ × 7½″	Side pockets
	1 @ 7½″ × 13½″	Back pocket
Fusible interfacing	1 @ 5″ × 13½″	Bottom
	2 @ 5″ × 9½″	Sides
	2 @ 9½″ × 13½″	Front and back

Travel Tote

Diaper Tote

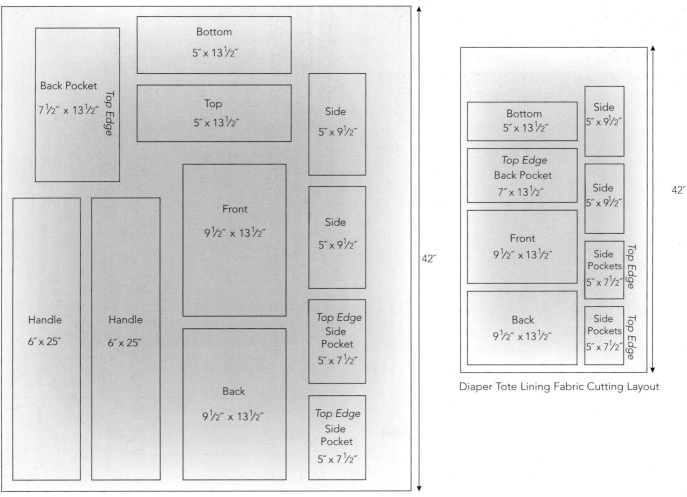

Diaper Tote Decorator Fabric Cutting Layout

Diaper Tote Lining Fabric Cutting Layout

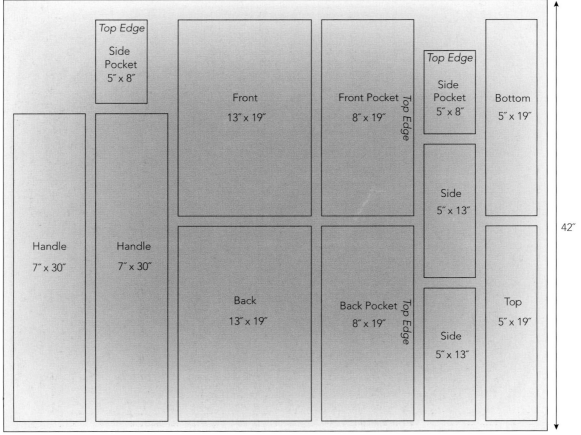

Travel Tote Decorator Fabric Cutting Layout

Cutting
Travel Tote

MATERIALS	CUTTING	FOR
Decorator fabric	2 @ 5″ x 19″	Bottom and top
	2 @ 5″ x 13″	Sides
	2 @ 13″ x 19″	Front and back
	2 @ 7″ x 30″	Handles
	2 @ 5″ x 8″	Side pockets
	2 @ 8″ x 19″	Front and back pockets
Lining fabric	1 @ 5″ x 19″	Bottom
	2 @ 5″ x 13″	Sides
	2 @ 13″ x 19″	Front and back
	2 @ 5″ x 8″	Side pockets
	2 @ 8″ x 19″	Front and back pockets
Fusible interfacing	1 @ 5″ x 19″	Bottom
	2 @ 5″ x 13″	Sides
	2 @ 13″ x 19″	Front and back

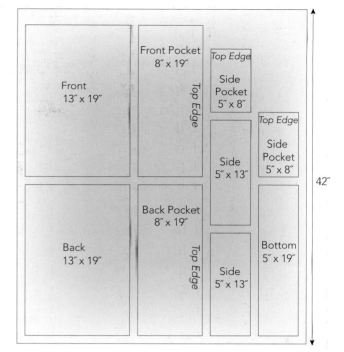

Travel Tote Lining Fabric Cutting Layout

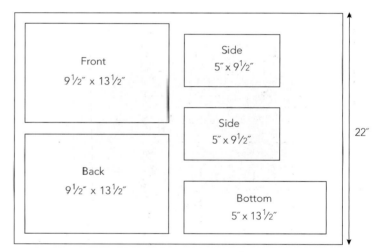

Diaper Tote Fusible Interfacing Cutting Layout

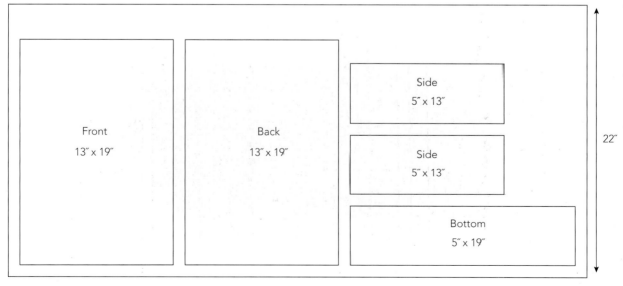

Travel Tote Fusible Interfacing Cutting Layout

Assembly

Seam allowances are ½".

1. Iron the fusible interfacing to the wrong side of the corresponding bottom, front, and back pieces of decorator fabric.

2. Make a Clean Finished-Edge Hem (page 15) on the top edge of each decorator fabric pocket and on the top edge of each lining fabric pocket.

3. Pin the decorator fabric side pockets to the decorator fabric sides of the bag, right sides up. Pin the decorator fabric front and back pockets to the decorator fabric front and back of the bag. Repeat with the lining fabric.

Note: The diaper bag does not have a front pocket in the lining or on the outside.

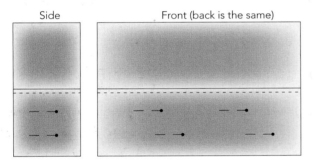

Pin pockets.

4. To divide the front and back pockets, measure 6˝ from each side edge, and use a chalk pencil to draw a line from the top to the bottom of the pocket. Topstitch on these lines. Back tack at the top of the pocket to secure.

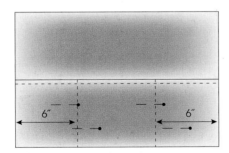

Measure and stitch to divide pockets.

Note: Be sure to back tack at the starting and stopping points as you are stitching the bag and the pocket pieces together.

5. Pin one of the side lining pieces to the back lining piece, right sides together. The Clean Finished-Edge Hems of the pockets should line up on the inside. Start stitching ½" from the top, and stop stitching ½" from the bottom edge. It is useful to mark the stop and start points, as the more accurate you are, the better the tote will fit together.

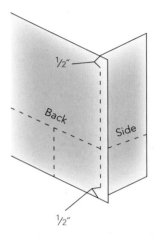

Start and stop stitching ½" from corners.

6. Pin the remaining side lining piece to the other side of the back lining, right sides together. Start stitching ½" from the top, and stop stitching ½" from the bottom edge.

7. One at a time, pin the sides to the front lining, right sides together. Start stitching ½" from each top edge, and stop stitching ½" from each bottom edge. You will now have a rectangular box shape.

8. With the lining inside out, pin the lining bottom piece to the front piece, right sides together. Stitch together, starting and ending ½" from each corner. Be as accurate as possible with the stitching so that the corners of the lining will fit properly into the outer bag.

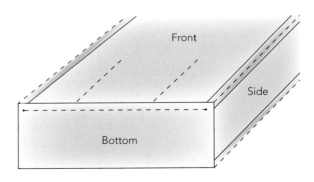

Stitch lining bottom.

9. Repeat Step 8 to stitch the bottom to the back piece and then to the sides. The seamlines should meet at the corners. Take your time to ensure that the fabric doesn't get caught in the stitches. Turn the lining right side out.

10. Repeat Steps 5–9 with the decorator fabric to assemble the outside of the tote. Take your time when making the outside—it will be a little bit more cumbersome with the fusible interfacing attached to the fabric. Once the outside of the tote is finished, trim the tips of the corners so the tote will sit better. Keep the outside of the tote inside out.

11. Make the handles using the Clean Edge Band technique (page 15). Topstitch ⅛″ from the edge on each side of one handle, and then repeat for the other handle.

12. To add the zipper to the tote top, cut the top piece of the decorator fabric in half lengthwise. Press one long edge on each strip under ¼″. Center one of the pressed-under edges over the zipper tape, and pin it in place. Work with the fabric and the zipper right side up.

Pressed-Under Edge of Top

½ of Top

Pin zipper.

13. Use a zipper foot to stitch along the folded edge of the fabric. You will need to unzip the zipper to get the foot past, and then zip it back up.

14. Pin and stitch the folded edge of the remaining top strip to the opposite side of the zipper.

15. Place one handle inside the front of the outside (decorator fabric) of the tote. For the Travel Tote, measure 5″ from each side seam, and pin the handle ends to the top of the tote with raw edges even. (For the Diaper Bag, measure in 3″.) Repeat to pin the remaining handle to the back of the tote.

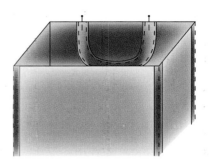

Pin handles to tote.

16. Place the inside-out decorator fabric tote inside the right-side-out lining with the sides seams aligned and the upper edges even. Pin in place with the wrong sides of the tote and lining together.

17. You will be stitching the top onto the tote in the same way that you stitched the bottom to the tote. **Unzip the zipper before starting so you can turn the tote right side out.** Pin the top to the front and back of the tote, and then to the sides. When pinning the ends of the zipper, make sure that you pin as if the zipper were closed.

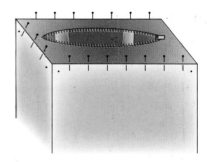

Pin before stitching.

18. Stitch the top to the tote and to the lining along each edge, starting and stopping the stitching ½″ from the corners. Use a zigzag stitch to finish the edges of the seam allowances together—this will keep the raw edge from unraveling inside your bag.

19. Turn the tote right side out, and push out the corners.

slumber party backpack

Remember the slumber parties you went to when you were growing up? Playing dress up and truth or dare. Staying up way past bedtime just talking. Feeling so homesick that sometimes you just had to have Mom or Dad come pick you up. When your kids are ready for slumber parties, send them off with this lined backpack you made just for them. The Slumber Party Backpack is big enough to hold the necessities, easy to carry with backpack straps, and so simple to make.

Basic Sewing Techniques

- Clean Edge Band
- Topstitch

Materials

MATERIALS	YARDAGE	FOR
Cotton print	1 yard	Outside of backpack and straps
Cotton fabric	½ yard	Lining
Ribbon	1¾ yards	Drawstring
Stitching and knitting gauge (optional)		

Cutting

MATERIALS	CUTTING	FOR
Cotton print	1 @ 14½″ × 41″	Outside of backpack
	2 @ 7″ × 21½″*	Straps
Cotton fabric	1 @ 14½″ × 41″	Lining

Before cutting the straps, make sure this strap length will fit your child. Adjust as needed.

FINISHED SIZE: 13½″ × 20¼″

Assembly

Seam allowances are ¼".

1. Measure and press under ¼" on the short edges of the outside fabric and the lining fabric. Set aside.

2. Measure and press under ¼" on the short edges of the straps.

3. Make the straps as a Clean Edge Band (page 15). Topstitch (page 11) around 3 sides of each strap ⅛" from the edge. Start and stop stitching at the folded edge, and pivot at the corners. Back tack at the starting and stopping points.

Fold

⅛"

Topstitch straps.

4. Fold the outside fabric in half crosswise, right sides together, with the pressed hems at the top. To mark the drawstring casing, measure down 1½" from the top edge, and make a pencil mark. Measure down 2½" from the top edge, and make another mark. Flip over the folded piece, and repeat on the other side.

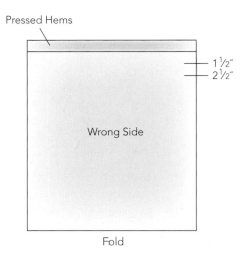

Pressed Hems

1½"
2½"

Wrong Side

Fold

Mark drawstring casing.

5. Unfold the outside fabric. To place the straps, measure 4¾" in from the side and 6" down from the top. Pin one end of each strap in place, as shown.

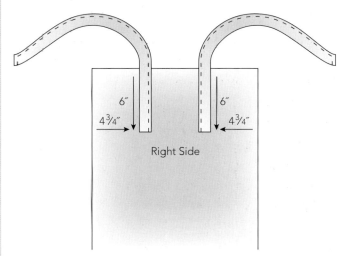

6"   6"
4¾"   4¾"

Right Side

Strap Placement

6. Topstitch the end of each strap in place securely.

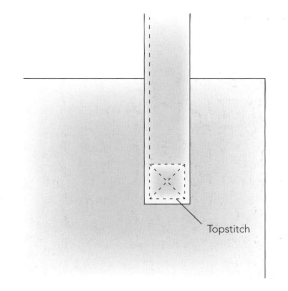

Topstitch

Topstitch straps.

7. Fold the outside fabric in half. Measure in 2″ from the side edge and 1″ up from the folded bottom edge. Pin the bottom ends of the straps in place at an angle as shown. Pin through the top layer only. Unfold and securely topstitch the bottom of the straps in place.

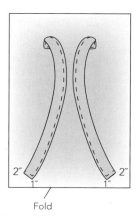

Unfold to topstitch bottom of straps.

8. Fold the outside fabric in half crosswise, **right** sides together. Securely pin the edges together so they don't slip. To stitch each side seam, start at the top edge with a back tack, and stitch to the 1½″ mark. Back tack at the stopping point. Lift the presser foot, back tack at the 2½″ mark, and stitch to the folded edge. Back tack. Press the seams open. Do not turn right side out.

9. Fold the lining fabric in half crosswise, right sides together. Stitch the side seams. Press the seams open. Turn right side out.

10. Place the inside-out backpack in the right-side-out lining with wrong sides together and side seams matching. Line up the top edges, and pin at the side seams and at the middle of each side. Topstitch around the top of the bag, ⅛″ from the edge.

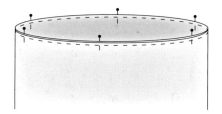

Topstitch around top of bag.

11. Turn the backpack right side out. Measure down 1½″ from the top, and stitch around the backpack.

12. Measure down 2½″ from the top, and again stitch around the backpack. This makes the casing for the backpack's drawstring.

Tip

Place a piece of tape on the machine to use as a guide when stitching the drawstring casing, or use a chalk pencil to mark around the entire bag.

13. Cut the ribbon in half, so you have 2 pieces for drawstrings. Fasten a safety pin to one end of a piece of ribbon. Push the closed safety pin through the opening in one side seam, working it through the casing and back out through the same opening. Remove the pin from the ribbon, and pull until the ribbon ends are even. Repeat to thread the remaining ribbon through the casing from the opposite side opening.

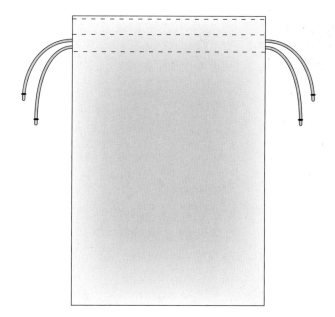

Ribbon Drawstrings

14. Pull both ends of the ribbons to close the bag.

Pack pajamas and a toothbrush. Add a little stuffed animal, and send your special someone off with a gift made by you!

wine gift bag

You got a last-minute invitation to a dinner party—tonight—and you have to take a hostess gift. Now what? Make a wine gift bag—it's simple, it's classy, and it's quick. Complete with a pocket on the front to place a gift tag, just to say thank you for the invite. You will leave your hostess speechless.

Basic Sewing Techniques

- Clean Finished-Edge Hem
- Topstitch

Materials

MATERIALS	YARDAGE	FOR
Cotton print	¼ yard	Outside
Cotton solid	¼ yard	Lining and pocket
Ribbon	1¼ yards	Drawstring
Chalk pencil		
Stitching and knitting gauge (optional)		

Cutting

MATERIALS	CUTTING	FOR
Cotton print	6½″ × 33½″	Outside
Cotton solid	6½″ × 33½″	Lining
	3½″ × 4½″	Pocket

FINISHED SIZE: 6˝ × 16½˝

Assembly

Seam allowances are ¼˝.

1. Measure and press under ¼˝ on the side and bottom edges of the pocket. Make a Clean Finished-Edge Hem (page 15) on the top edge of the pocket. Set aside.

2. Press under ¼˝ on the short edges of the outside fabric and the lining.

3. Center the pocket on the outside fabric piece, right sides up, 7˝ from the top. Pin the pocket in place.

Press under edge.

7˝

Pocket Placement

4. Topstitch (page 11) the sides and bottom of the pocket to the outside fabric ⅛″ from the edges. Back tack at the starting and stopping points.

5. Fold the outside fabric in half crosswise with right sides together and with the pressed ¼″ hems at the top. Pin the side edges together. To mark the drawstring casing on the wrong side of the fabric, measure down 1″ from the top edge, and make a pencil mark. Measure down 2″ from the top edge, and make another pencil mark. Flip over the folded fabric, and repeat on the other side.

Mark drawstring casing.

6. To stitch each side seam, start at the top edge with a back tack, stitch to the 1″ mark, and back tack. Lift the presser foot, back tack at the 2″ mark, and stitch to the folded edge. Back tack. Press the seams open. Do not turn the bag right side out.

7. Fold the lining in half crosswise, right sides together, and pin securely. Begin at the top edge, and stitch each side seam. Back tack at the starting and stopping points. Press the seams open. Turn right side out.

8. Place the inside-out outside bag in the right-side-out lining with wrong sides together and side seams matching. Line up the folded top edges, and pin at the side seams and at the middle of each side.

Pin top of bag.

9. Topstitch around the bag top ⅛″ from the edge, catching the edges of the folded hems in the stitching. Turn right side out.

10. Measure down 1″ from the top, and stitch around the bag.

11. Measure down 2″ from the top, and again stitch around the bag. This makes the casing for the drawstring on the bag.

Tip

Place a piece of tape on the machine to use as a guide when stitching the drawstring casing, or use a chalk pencil to mark around the entire bag.

12. Cut the ribbon in half, so you have 2 pieces for drawstrings. Fasten a safety pin to one end of a piece of ribbon. Push the closed safety pin through the opening in one side seam, working it through the casing and back out through the same opening. Remove the pin from the ribbon, and pull until the ribbon ends are even. Repeat to thread the remaining ribbon through the casing from the opposite side opening.

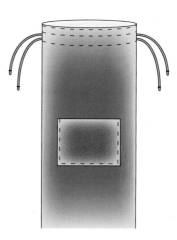

Ribbon drawstrings

Have a great time at the dinner party!

cosmetic bag with pockets

Don't you hate digging through your cosmetic bag trying to find lipstick, mascara, or a shadow brush? So do we! We put pockets on the inside of this handy little bag, so you can find all that little stuff that ends up on the bottom of the bag. Make a bunch of these bags as gifts for all your friends. Better yet, throw a Cosmetic Bag Party. Your friends can make bags themselves, and you can spend the evening getting caught up and embellishing bags.

Basic Sewing Techniques

- Clean Finished-Edge Hem
- Topstitch

FINISHED SIZE: 6½″ × 11″

Materials

MATERIALS	YARDAGE	FOR
Cotton print	¼ yard	Outside
Cotton solid	¼ yard	Lining and pocket
Ribbon	1¼ yards	Drawstring
Chalk pencil		
Stitching and knitting gauge (optional)		

Cutting

MATERIALS	CUTTING	FOR
Cotton print	7½″ × 22½″	Outside
Cotton solid	7½″ × 22½″	Lining
	7½″ × 12″	Inside pocket

Assembly

Seam allowances are ¼".

1. Measure and press under ¼" on the short edges of the outside fabric and the lining.

2. Make a Clean Finished-Edge Hem (page 15) on the short edges of the pocket.

3. Center the pocket on the lining, with both pieces right side up, the side edges aligned, and pin in place. Measure 1¾" from each side edge of the pocket, and use a chalk pencil to draw a line from the top to the bottom of each side of the pocket. Repeat to draw a center line 2" in from the outside lines. Topstitch (page 11) on these lines. Back tack at the start and stop of each stitching line.

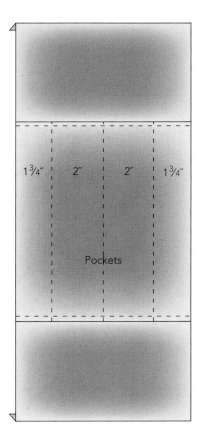

1¾" 2" 2" 1¾"

Pockets

Pocket Placement and Stitching Lines

4. Fold the lining in half crosswise, right sides together, and pin securely. Begin at the top edge, and stitch each side seam. Back tack at the starting and stopping points. Press the seams open. Turn right side out.

5. Fold the outside fabric in half crosswise with right sides together and the pressed ¼" hems at the top. Pin the edges together. To mark the drawstring casing, measure down 1" from the top edge, and make a pencil mark on the wrong side of the fabric. Measure down 2" from the top edge, and make another pencil mark. Flip over the folded fabric, and repeat on the other side.

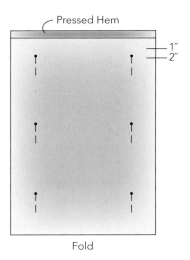

Pressed Hem

1"
2"

Fold

Mark drawstring casing.

6. To stitch each side seam on the outside fabric, start at the top edge, and stitch to the 1" mark. Back tack at the starting and stopping point. Lift the presser foot, back tack at the 2" mark, and stitch to the folded edge. Back tack. Press the seams open. Do not turn right side out.

7. Place the inside-out outside fabric in the right-side-out lining with wrong sides together and side seams matching. Line up the top edges, and pin at the side seams and at the middle of each side.

Pin top of bag.

8. Topstitch around the top of the bag ⅛″ from the edge, catching the edge of the hem in the stitching. Turn right side out.

9. Measure down 1″ from the top, and stitch around the bag.

10. Measure down 2″ from the top, and again stitch around the bag. This makes the casing for the drawstring on the bag.

Tip

Place a piece of tape on the machine to use as a guide when stitching the drawstring casing, or use a chalk pencil to mark around the entire bag.

11. Cut the ribbon in half, so you have 2 pieces for drawstrings. Fasten a safety pin to one end of a piece of ribbon. Push the closed safety pin through the opening in one side seam, working it through the casing and back out through the same opening. Remove the pin from the ribbon, and pull until the ribbon ends are even. Repeat to thread the remaining ribbon through the casing from the opposite side opening.

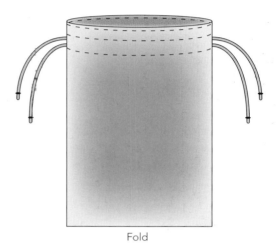

Fold

Ribbon Drawstrings

12. Pull both ends of the ribbons to close the bag.

grocery totes

With today's emphasis on recycling, more and more people are using fabric bags for groceries. When you create your own, you can make it uniquely yours. We selected Osnaberg, a heavier-weight cotton, for this project. The fabric makes the bag sturdy for all of your shopping needs, and the striped lining adds a decorative touch. Of course, you can use the bag any way you like. Take it to the beach, or use it for your knitting. Personalize the bag with simple Big-Stitch Embroidery. We have included two versions of this bag, one plain and one with a decorative band. Save the environment and make several.

FINISHED SIZES:

EMBROIDERED TOTE:
17″ × 18½″

DECORATIVE BAND
TOTE: 17″ × 18½″

Basic Sewing Techniques

- Clean Edge Band

- Big-Stitch Embroidery

- Topstitch

Materials

MATERIALS	YARDAGE	FOR
Heavy-weight cotton*	⅝ yard	Outside (Embroidered Tote)
Cotton fabric	⅞ yard	Lining and handles (Embroidered Tote)
OR		
Heavy-weight cotton*	⅝ yard	Outside (Decorative Band Tote)
Cotton fabric	1⅛ yards	Lining, band, and handles (Decorative Band Tote)
Six-strand embroidery floss or perle cotton		
Embroidery needle		

* Use Osnaberg, canvas, denim, or decorator fabric.

Cutting

MATERIALS	CUTTING	FOR
Heavy-weight cotton	1 @ 19″ × 38″	Outside (Embroidered Tote)
Cotton fabric	1 @ 19″ × 38″	Lining (Embroidered Tote)
	2 @ 4″ × 25″	Handles (Embroidered Tote)
OR		
Heavy-weight cotton	1 @ 19″ × 38″	Outside (Decorative Band Tote)
Cotton fabric	1 @ 19″ × 40″	Lining (Decorative Band Tote)
	2 @ 4″ × 30″	Handles (Decorative Band Tote)
	2 @ 4″ × 19″	Bands (Decorative Band Tote)

Assembly

Seam allowances are ½″.

Embroidered Tote

1. Fold the outside fabric in half crosswise right side out to determine the embroidery placement. Mark the area that you are going to embroider with tape. Use Big-Stitch Embroidery (page 12) to embroider the word "Grocery." We handwrote the letters 2″ tall with a pencil.

2. Fold the outside fabric in half crosswise, right sides together, and press.

3. Stitch each side seam using a ½″ seam allowance. Back tack at the starting and stopping points.

4. Open the tote bottom and place the pressed line on the bottom of the tote with the side seam. Measure 3″ down from the corner point, and draw a line from edge to edge as shown. Stitch on the drawn line. Repeat on the other side of the bag. Trim off the excess corners, leaving a ½″ seam allowance. Press the seams open.

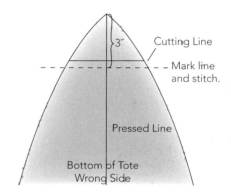

Fold with pressed line even with side seam.

5. Turn the bag right side out, and press under ½″ on the top edge.

6. Repeat Steps 2–5 for the lining. Do not turn the lining right side out.

7. Make the handles with a Clean Edge Band (page 15). Topstitch ⅛″ from the edge on each side of one handle, and then repeat for the other handle.

8. Put the inside-out lining into the right-side-out bag with wrong sides together and with the side seams and the top edges even. Pin at the side seams.

9. Measure in 5″ from the side seams, and insert the handle ends between the lining and the outside of the bag. Pin the handle in place. Repeat on the opposite side of the bag. Pin together the top edges of the bag and the lining.

10. Use contrasting thread to topstitch (page 11) around the top of the bag, first ⅛″ from the edge and again ½″ from the edge. Push the lining into the bottom corners of the bag. Pinch the bag and lining fabric together at the bottom edge, and topstitch ⅛″ from the bottom edge.

Topstitch top and bottom of bag.

Decorative Band Tote

1. Measure and press under ½″ on the long edges of both band strips.

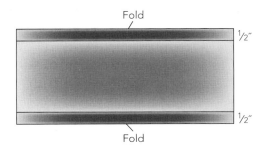

Create decorative bands.

2. Fold the outside fabric in half crosswise, right sides together, and press.

3. Unfold the bag. Measure down 6″ from the top raw edge, and pin a band strip across the right side of the bag. Repeat on the other side.

4. Topstitch (page 11) the band onto the bag ⅛″ from the edge of the band. Repeat Steps 2–6 of the Embroidered Tote for bag construction. However, follow Step 5 below for folding the top edge of the lining.

5. Turn the lining wrong side out. Press under 1″ and then another 1″ to the wrong side to create the decorative band at the top of the bag.

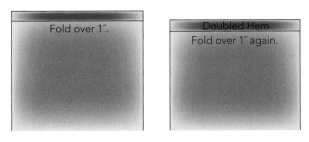

Fold lining.

6. Place the lining in the bag with wrong sides together and side seams matching. Place the folded top edge of the lining on the outside of the bag. Pin at the side seams.

7. Make handles with a Clean Edge Band (page 15).

8. Topstitch ⅛″ from the edge on each side of one handle, and then repeat for the other handle.

9. Measure in 5″ from each side seam. Insert the handle under the lining band. Fold the handle up over the lining band and pin.

10. Use contrasting thread to topstitch around the top of the bag, first ⅛″ from the top edge and again ½″ from the top edge. Push the lining into the bottom corners of the bag. Pinch the bag and lining fabric together at the bottom edge, and topstitch in ⅛″.

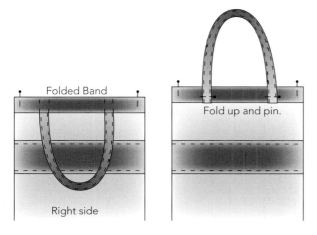

Folded Band

Right side

Pin handles in place.

Fold up and pin.

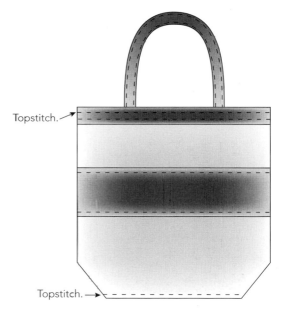

Topstitch.

Topstitch.

Topstitch top and bottom of bag.

Head out to the farmers' market, and fill your bag with dinner.

stylishly accessorized

piped-edge pillows

Pillows warm a setting, bringing softness and comfort while adding a stylish accent to any room. We offer two very simple styles—the Long Couch Pillow and the Personalized Embroidered Pillow. The Personalized Embroidered Pillow is a perfect gift for a special friend or a baby shower, or you can monogram one for yourself. Add your touch, sit back, and enjoy a little extra comfort.

Basic Sewing Techniques

- Piping
- Pillows With Piping
- Big-Stitch Embroidery
- Whipstitch

Materials
Long Couch Pillow

MATERIALS	YARDAGE	FOR
Cotton fabric 1	½ yard	Front
Cotton fabric 2	1 yard	Piping and back
Cotton cording	2¾ yards	Piping
Pillow form	28″ × 14″	

FINISHED SIZES:

LONG COUCH PILLOW: 28″ × 14″

PERSONALIZED EMBROIDERED PILLOW: 22″ × 12″

Personalized Embroidered Pillow

MATERIALS	YARDAGE	FOR
Cotton fabric 1	½ yard	Front
Cotton fabric 2	1 yard	Piping and back
Cotton cording	2⅓ yards	Piping
Pillow form	22″ × 12″	
Six-strand embroidery floss in contrasting accent color		
Embroidery needle		
Chalk pencil		
2 buttons (optional)		
Long doll needle (optional, if adding a button to the center)		
Heavy-weight thread (optional, if adding a button to the center)		

Cutting
Long Couch Pillow

MATERIALS	CUTTING	FOR
Cotton fabric 1	14½″ × 28½″	Front
Cotton fabric 2	14½″ × 28½″	Back
	See page 13	Bias strips for piping

Personalized Embroidered Pillow

MATERIALS	CUTTING	FOR
Cotton fabric 1	12½″ × 22½″	Front
Cotton fabric 2	12½″ × 22½″	Back
	See page 13	Bias strips for piping

Assembly

Seam allowances are ¼″.

1. To make the Long Couch Pillow, refer to Piping (pages 13–14) and Pillows With Piping (page 14) to make bias strips and piping, and to assemble the pillow.   **OR**

To make the Personalized Embroidered Pillow, use Big-Stitch Embroidery (page 12) to embroider the pillow panels. Then refer to Piping (pages 13–14) and Pillows With Piping (page 14) to make bias strips and piping, and to assemble the pillow.

2. When stitching the pillow front to the back, remember to leave an opening for inserting the pillow form. To do this, you will be leaving one short edge open: Stitch, starting and stopping approximately 1″ around 2 adjacent corners. Remember to back tack each of these starting and stopping points to secure the stitches.

3. Turn the pillow right side out. Gently squish the pillow form into the pillow cover. Whipstitch (page 11) the opening closed.

4. To add a button to the center of the pillow, use 1 button on the front, and 1 button on the back. Thread the doll needle with a long length of heavy-weight thread and knot the thread. From the back side of the pillow, stitch up through the center front of the pillow, and through the holes or shank of the button. Stitch through the pillow to the back, and through the holes or shank of the 2nd button. Pull the thread to indent the pillow. Repeat several times for strength. Knot the thread securely under the button on the back of the pillow.

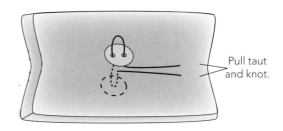

Pull taut and knot.

Give the gift of comfort, or cozy up on the couch with your new pillows.

throws

These easy-to-make throws add warmth, style, and comfort to any room. Make a His-and-Hers Throw or a smaller Personalized Baby Throw. The simple design allows you to personalize either throw with Big-Stitch Embroidery. Add a twist with a contemporary motif, a monogram, or just a few straight stitches. Make the throw from solids, or choose an eclectic mixture of color and textures by using several prints, including a geometric-style fabric. Give the His-and-Hers Throw as a gift to newlyweds. The Personalized Baby Throw is the perfect baby shower gift.

FINISHED SIZES:

HIS-AND-HERS THROW: 58″ × 65″

PERSONALIZED BABY THROW: 30″ × 50″

Basic Sewing Techniques

- Big-Stitch Embroidery
- Whipstitch
- Topstitch

Materials
His-and-Hers Throw

MATERIALS	YARDAGE	FOR
Cotton fabric 1	1⅝ yards	Main theme print
Cotton fabric 2	1 yard	Top border
Cotton fabric 3	1⅝ yards	Side border
Cotton fabric 4	3⅝ yards	Backing
Batting	62″ × 69″	
Six-strand embroidery floss		Big-Stitch Embroidery
Embroidery needle		
Thread in an accent color		Topstitching

Personalized Baby Throw

MATERIALS	YARDAGE	FOR
Cotton fabric 1	⅔ yard	Main theme print
Cotton fabric 2	⅜ yard	Top border
Cotton fabric 3	⅜ yard	Side border
Cotton fabric 4	1⅝ yards	Backing
Batting	34″ × 54″	
Six-strand embroidery floss		Big-Stitch Embroidery
Embroidery needle		
Thread in an accent color		Topstitching

Cutting

His-and-Hers Throw

MATERIALS	CUTTING	FOR
Cotton fabric 1	1 @ 33½″ × 50½″	Main theme print
Cotton fabric 2	2 @ 15½″ × 29½″	Top border
Cotton fabric 3	1 @ 25½″ × 50½″	Side border
Cotton fabric 4	2 @ 62″ × width of fabric	Backing (horizontal seam)

Personalized Baby Throw

MATERIALS	CUTTING	FOR
Cotton fabric 1	40½″ × 20½″	Main theme print
Cotton fabric 2	30½″ × 10½″	Top border
Cotton fabric 3	40½″ × 10½″	Side border
Cotton fabric 4	54″ × width of fabric	Backing

Assembly

Seam allowances are ¼".

1. Place the main theme fabric piece right sides together with the side border, and stitch. Press the seam open.

2. For the His-and-Hers Throw, place the short edges of the top border right sides together, and stitch. Press the seams open.

3. Place the top border piece right sides together with the main theme and side border unit, and stitch. Press the seam open.

4. For the His-and-Hers Throw, place the long edges of the backing pieces right sides together, and stitch. Press the seams open and set the backing aside.

5. Use Big-Stitch Embroidery (page 12) to personalize the throw with the Flower Pattern (page 75), a design copied from the main theme print, or initials, or create your own design.

6. Layer the pieced top and the backing fabric with right sides together. Trim the backing just slightly larger than the top. Cut the batting the same size as the backing.

7. Place the top and backing, right sides together, on top of the batting. Use straight pins to pin the layers together.

8. Stitch around the edge of the layered throw, using a ¼" seam allowance. Leave a 5"-wide opening in the center of the bottom edge.

9. Trim the backing and batting even with the pieced top, leaving a ¼" seam allowance. Trim the points from each corner. Be sure not to cut so close that you cut the stitching.

10. Turn the throw right side out. Push out each corner. Slide your fingers into the throw, and push the seams to the edges. Press, pressing under the seam allowances of the opening. Work your way around until all the edges are pressed.

11. Use a whipstitch (page 11) to stitch the opening closed.

12. Use a walking foot and a longer stitch length to stitch the layers together in a desired pattern. Use ½" allowance from all edges. Back tack at the starting and stopping points.

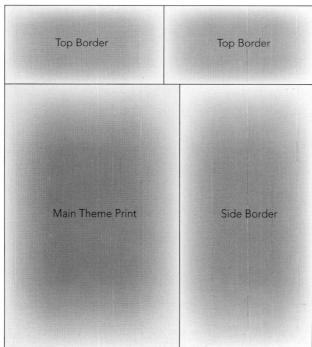

His-and-Hers Throw Fabric Layout

Flower Pattern

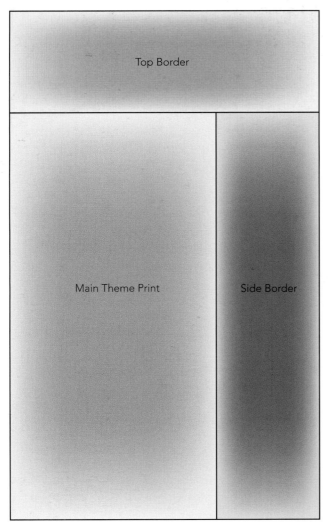

Top Border

Main Theme Print

Side Border

Personalized Baby Throw Fabric Layout

fabric foot stool

You see foot stools in catalogs, typically in leather or faux leather. They look fine in the catalog, but somehow they just don't work for you. Make a fabric foot stool to fit your needs, your colors, and your personality. Coordinate with your couch, pillows, and throws to add stylish comfort to your home.

Basic Sewing Technique

■ Whipstitch

Materials

MATERIALS	YARDAGE	FOR
Cotton print 1	1⅛ yards	Foot stool cover
Cotton print 2	1⅛ yards	Foot stool cover
Foam shape	18″ × 14″ × 14″	Inside

Cutting

MATERIALS	CUTTING	FOR
Cotton print 1	2 @ 19¼″ × 15¼″	Sides
	1 @ 15¼″ × 15¼″	Ends
Cotton print 2	2 @ 19¼″ × 15¼″	Sides
	1 @ 15¼″ × 15¼″	Ends

FINISHED SIZE: 18″ × 14″ × 14″

Assembly

Seam allowances are ¼″.

1. Cut each rectangle and square diagonally from corner to corner. Repeat in the other direction, creating 4 triangles from each square and rectangle for a total of 24 triangles.

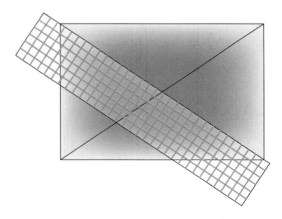

Cut squares and rectangles diagonally.

2. To make each side panel, sew together 4 triangles cut from the rectangles. Make 4 side panels. Press the seams.

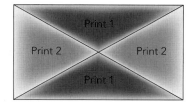

Sew together 4 triangles to make side panel. Make 4.

3. In a similar manner, make the end panels by sewing together the triangles cut from the squares.

4. Pin a pieced square and the short edge of a pieced rectangle with right sides together. Stitch together along the short edge. Repeat for a second rectangle and the remaining square.

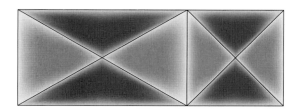

Stitch pieced square to pieced rectangle. Make 2.

5. Stitch one remaining rectangle to the edges of one assembled square/rectangle, stitching to the edge of the rectangle and then to the edge of the square. Start and stop stitching ¼″ from the corners. Back tack at the starting and stopping points.

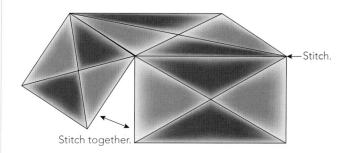

Stitch rectangle to assembled rectangle/square.

6. Repeat Step 5 to stitch the remaining rectangle to the other assembled rectangle/square.

7. Stitch the 2 sections together to form a rectangular box, leaving one long edge and an adjacent short edge open to insert the foam.

8. Turn the foot stool cover right side out and press, pressing under the seam allowances of the opening. Insert the foam.

9. Close the open edges with a whipstitch (page 11).

Place next to your favorite chair and relax.

ABOUT THE AUTHORS

Carolyn and Valori met at The Stitchin' Post as teenagers and have continued to work together over the years, becoming close friends and colleagues. Carolyn is an integral part of the creative style at Twigs Gifts and at The Stitchin' Post. Valori is a fabric designer, author, and co-owner of the businesses. Their forward thinking keeps the stores on the cutting edge of trends and styles in quilting, knitting, and home decorating. The collaboration on the projects in this book brings together their creativity and unique style.

Other books by Valori Wells

Books by Jean and Valori Wells

  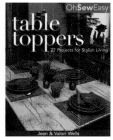

SOURCES

For a list of other fine books from C&T Publishing, ask for a free catalog:
C&T Publishing, Inc.
P.O. Box 1456
Lafayette, CA 94549
(800) 284-1114
Email: ctinfo@ctpub.com
Website: www.ctpub.com

C&T Publishing's professional photography services are now available to the public. Visit us at www.ctmediaservices.com.

QUILTING SUPPLIES

The Stitchin' Post
P.O. Box 280
311 W. Cascade
Sisters, OR 97759
(541) 549-6061
Website: www.stitchinpost.com

Cotton Patch
1025 Brown Ave.
Lafayette, CA 94549
(800) 835-4418 or
(925) 283-7883
Email: CottonPa@aol.com
Website: www.quiltusa.com

Note: Fabrics used in the quilts shown may not be currently available, as fabric manufacturers keep most fabrics in print for only a short time.

Great Titles
from C&T PUBLISHING

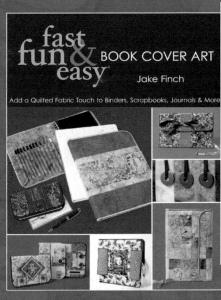

fast fun & easy
BOOK COVER ART
Jake Finch
Add a Quilted Fabric Touch to Binders, Scrapbooks, Journals & More

mix make it you

your space
Sew with Style | Easy Step-by-Step Instructions | Uniquely You
Shannon Mullen

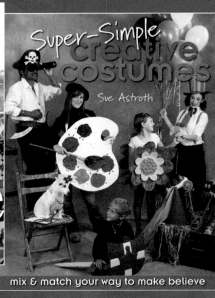

Super-Simple creative costumes
Sue Astroth
mix & match your way to make believe

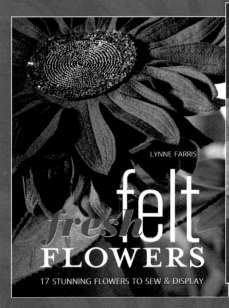

LYNNE FARRIS
fresh felt FLOWERS
17 STUNNING FLOWERS TO SEW & DISPLAY

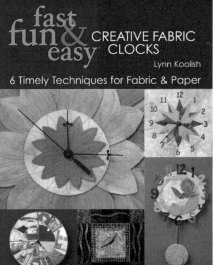

fast fun & easy
CREATIVE FABRIC CLOCKS
Lynn Koolish
6 Timely Techniques for Fabric & Paper

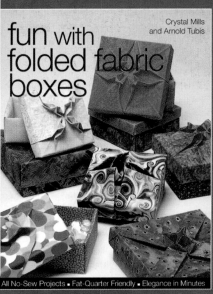

Crystal Mills and Arnold Tubis
fun with folded fabric boxes
All No-Sew Projects • Fat-Quarter Friendly • Elegance in Minutes

---

Available at your local retailer or
www.ctpub.com or 800.284.1114